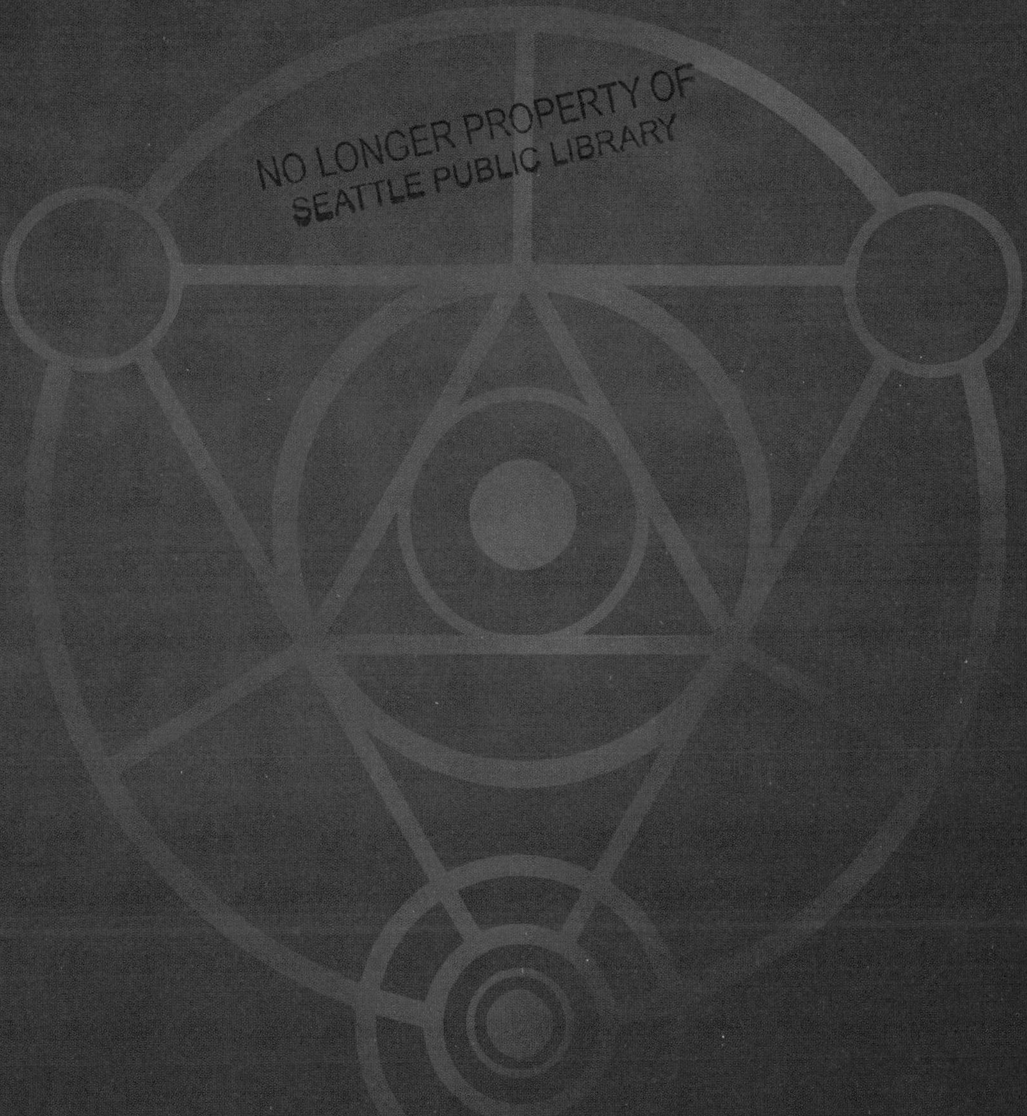

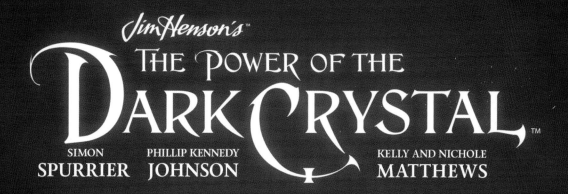

Jim Henson's
THE POWER OF THE
DARK CRYSTAL ™

SIMON
SPURRIER

PHILLIP KENNEDY
JOHNSON

KELLY AND NICHOLE
MATTHEWS

VOLUME THREE

Published by
ARCHAIA ™

Jim Henson's
THE POWER OF THE
DARK CRYSTAL ™

Based on screenplays by
Craig Pearce
And
Annette Duffy and **David Odell**

Written by **Simon Spurrier** and
Phillip Kennedy Johnson
Illustrated by **Kelly** and **Nichole Matthews**
Lettered by **Jim Campbell**

Cover by **Jae Lee** and **June Chung**
Chapter Break Art by **Sana Takeda**

Series Designer **Marie Krupina**
Collection Designer **Jillian Crab**
Assistant Editor **Gavin Gronenthal**
Editors **Cameron Chittock** and **Sierra Hahn**

Special Thanks to **Brian Henson**, **Lisa Henson**, **Jim Formanek**,
Nicole Goldman, **Maryanne Pittman**, **Carla DellaVedova**,
Justin Hilden, **Karen Falk**, **Blanca Lista**, **Wendy Froud**, **Brian Froud**,
Kelsey Dieterich, and the entire **Jim Henson Company** team.

Ross Richie CEO & Founder
Matt Gagnon Editor-in-Chief
Filip Sablik President of Publishing & Marketing
Stephen Christy President of Development
Lance Kreiter VP of Licensing & Merchandising
Phil Barbaro VP of Finance
Arune Singh VP of Marketing
Bryce Carlson Managing Editor
Scott Newman Production Design Manager
Kate Henning Operations Manager
Spencer Simpson Sales Manager
Sierra Hahn Senior Editor
Dafna Pleban Editor, Talent Development
Shannon Watters Editor
Eric Harburn Editor
Whitney Leopard Editor
Cameron Chittock Editor
Chris Rosa Associate Editor
Matthew Levine Associate Editor
Sophie Philips-Roberts Assistant Editor
Gavin Gronenthal Assistant Editor
Michael Moccio Assistant Editor
Amanda LaFranco Executive Assistant
Katalina Holland Editorial Administrative Assistant
Jillian Crab Design Coordinator
Michelle Ankley Design Coordinator
Kara Leopard Production Designer
Marie Krupina Production Designer
Grace Park Production Design Assistant
Chelsea Roberts Production Design Assistant
Elizabeth Loughridge Accounting Coordinator
Stephanie Hocutt Social Media Coordinator
José Meza Event Coordinator
Holly Aitchison Operations Coordinator
Megan Christopher Operations Assistant
Rodrigo Hernandez Mailroom Assistant
Morgan Perry Direct Market Representative
Cat O'Grady Marketing Assistant
Cornelia Tzana Publicity Assistant
Liz Almendarez Accounting Administrative Assistant

ARCHAIA™

BOOM! Studios, 5670 Wilshire Boulevard,
Suite 400, Los Angeles, CA 90036-5679.

Printed in China. First Printing.

ISBN: 978-1-68415-208-7
eISBN: 978-1-64144-023-3

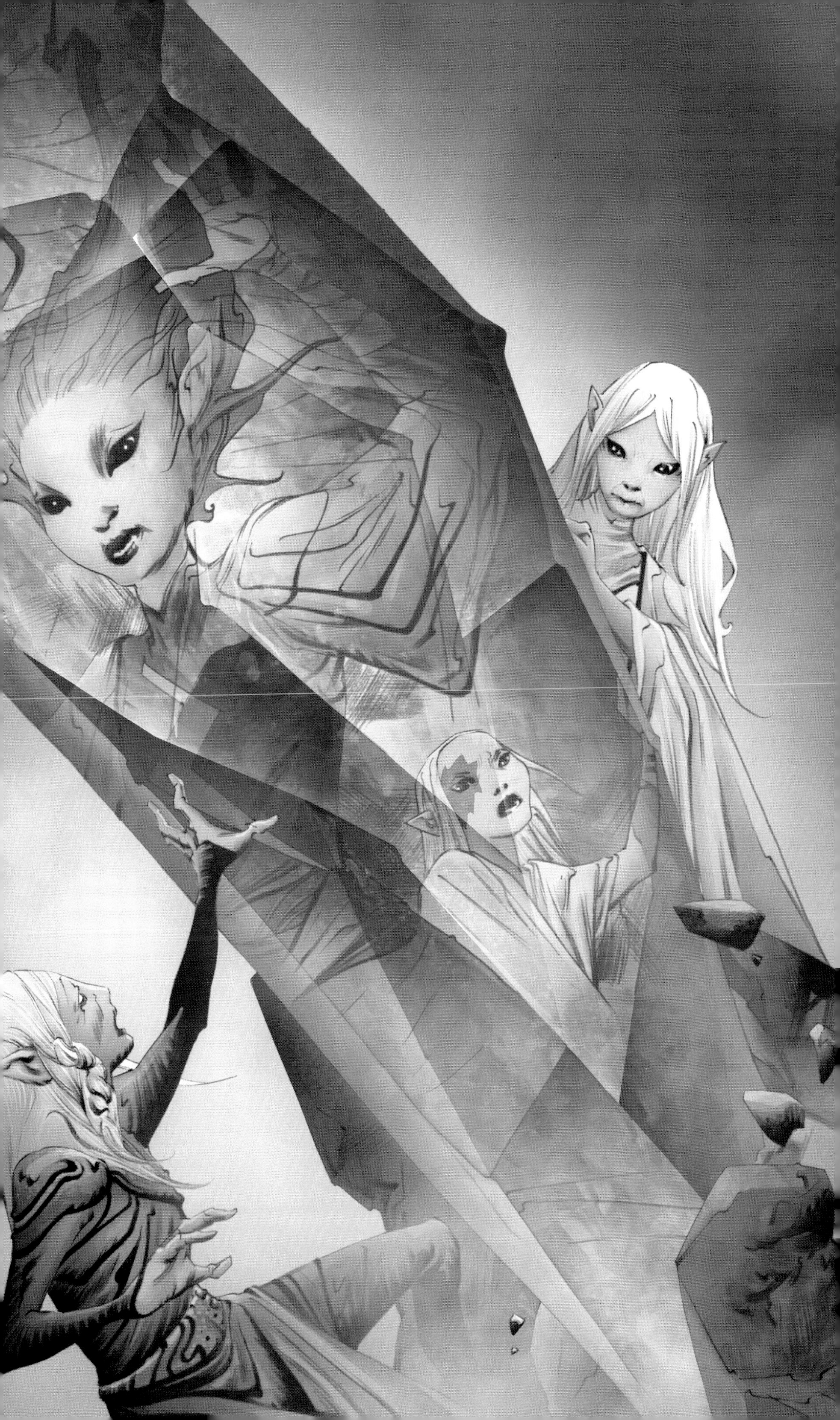

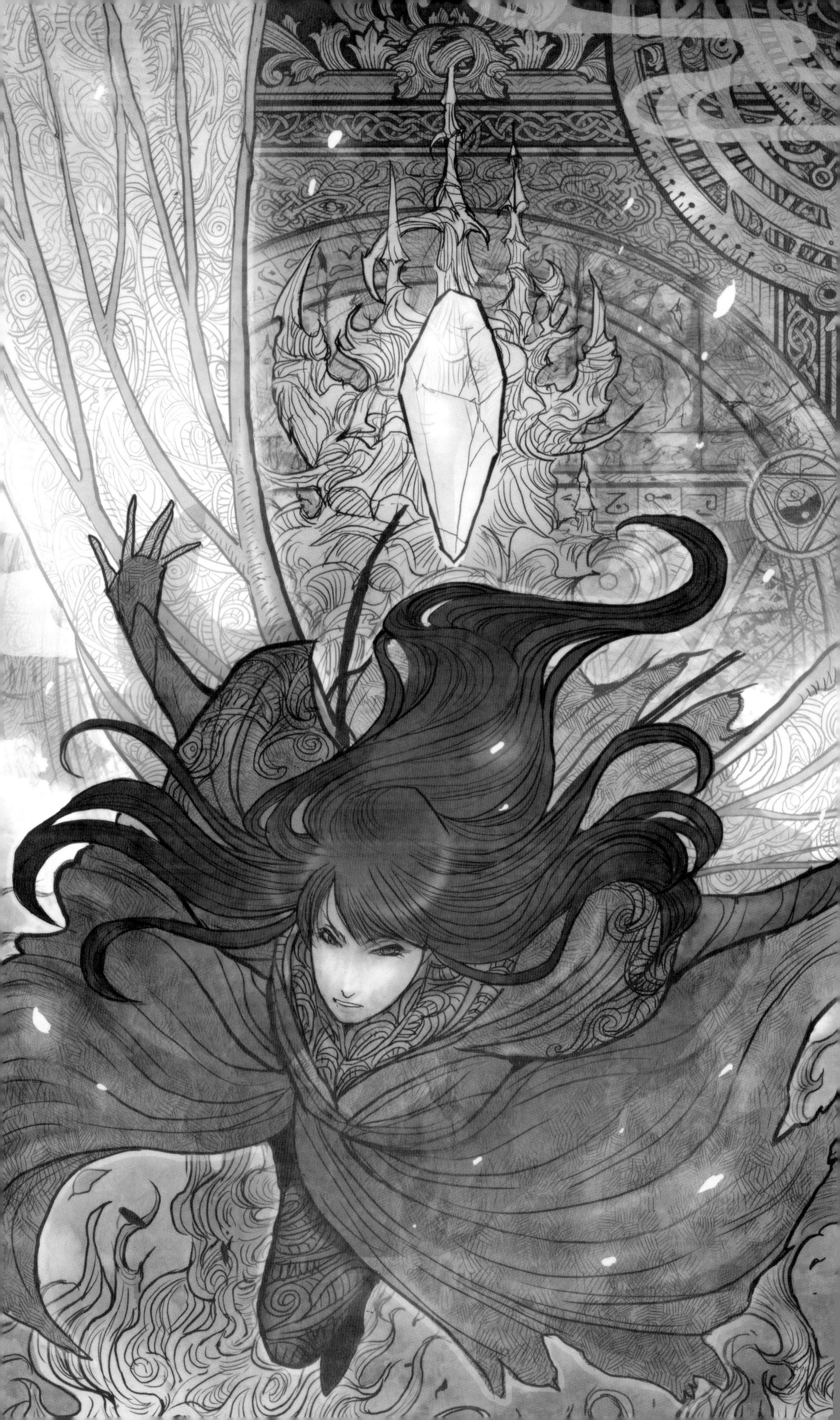

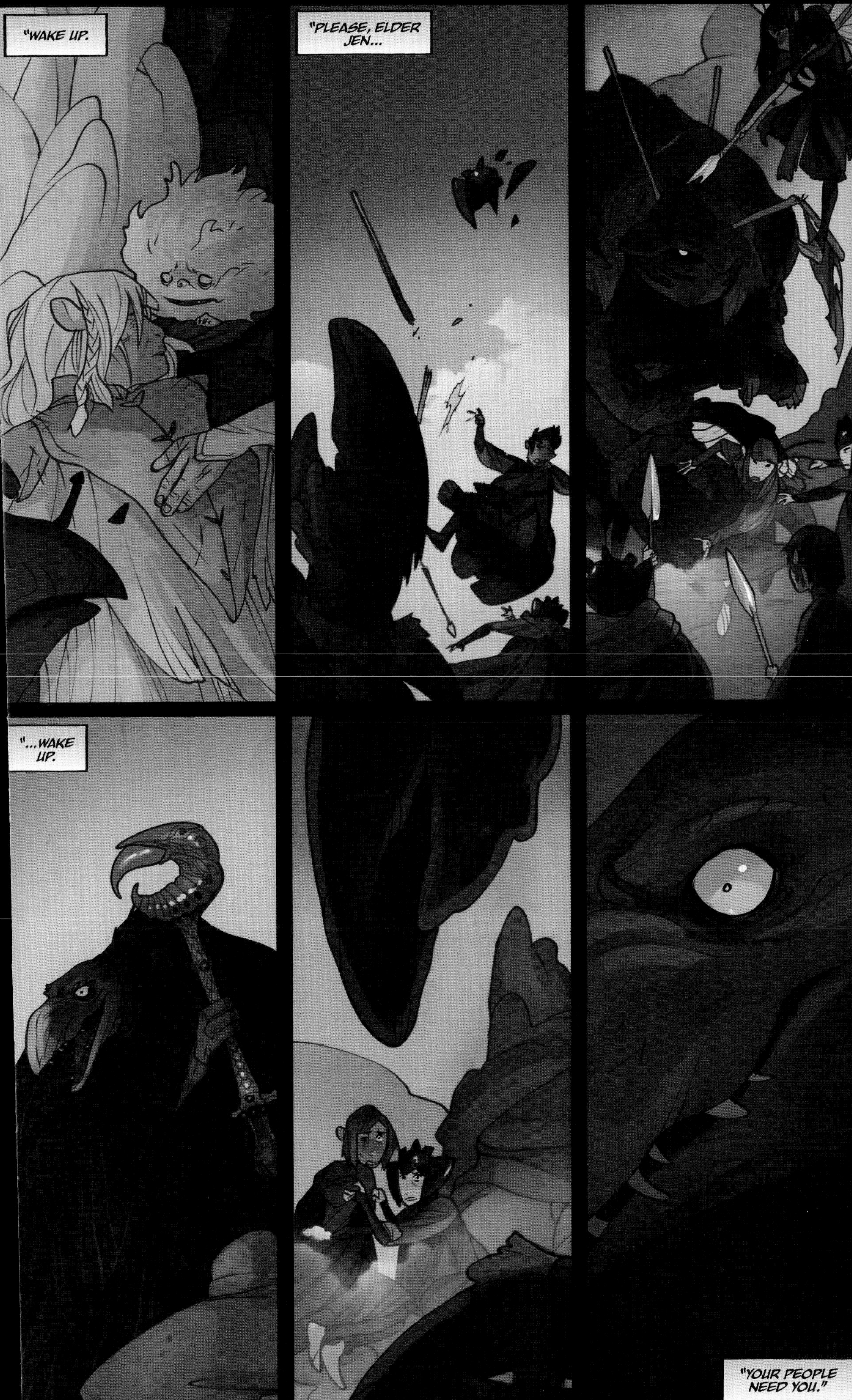
"WAKE UP.
"PLEASE, ELDER JEN...
"...WAKE UP.
"YOUR PEOPLE NEED YOU."

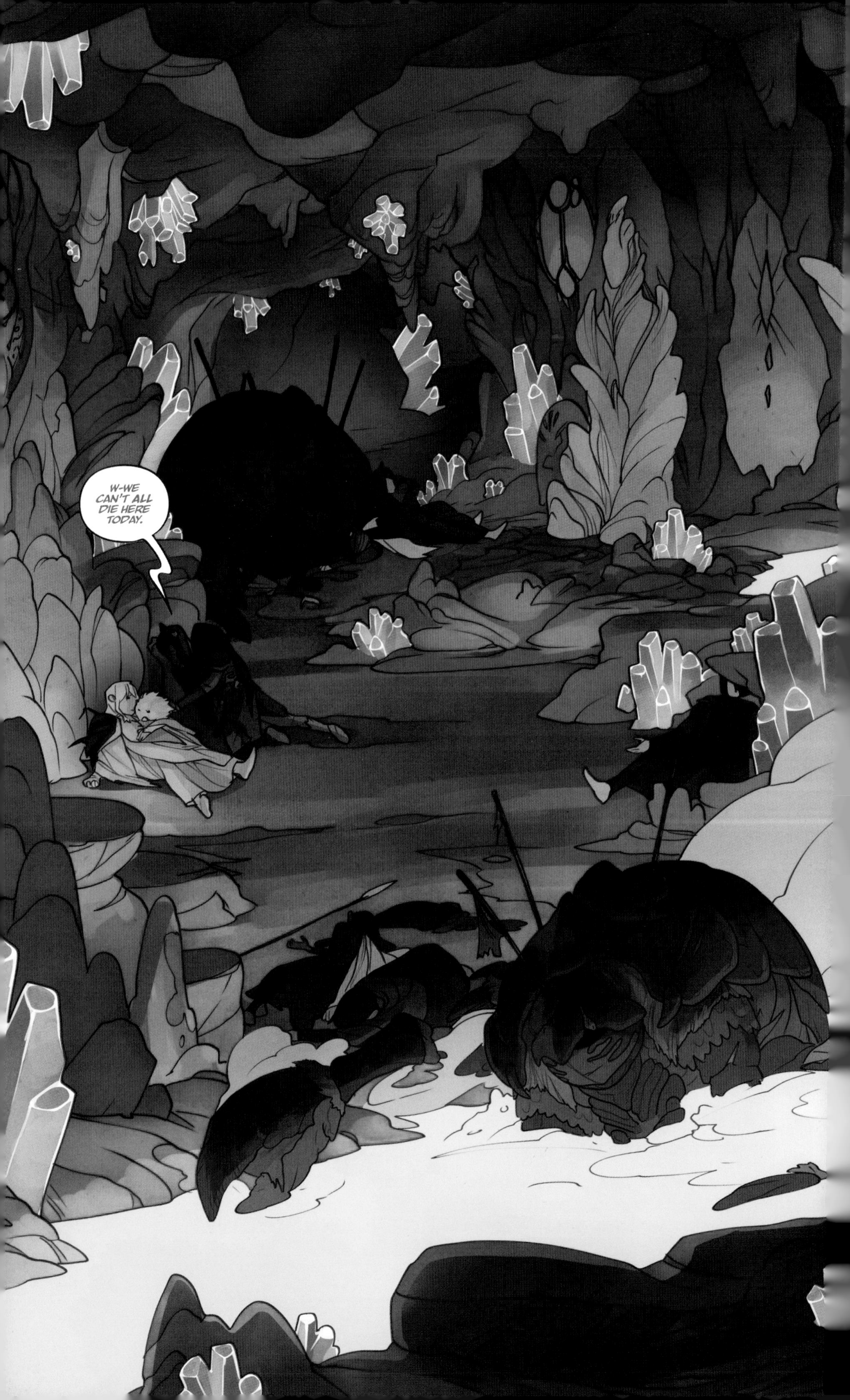
W-WE CAN'T ALL DIE HERE TODAY.

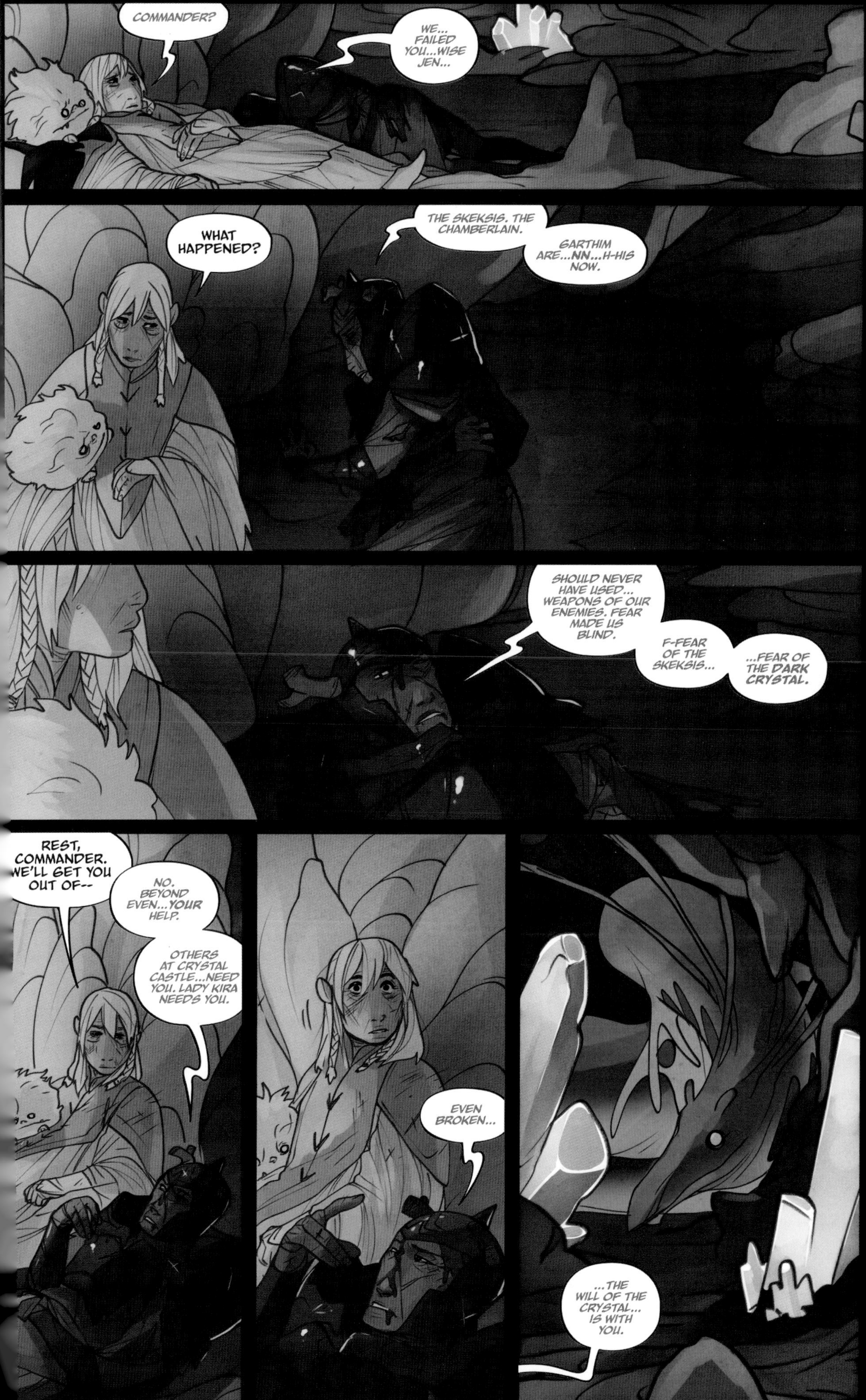
COMMANDER?
WE... FAILED YOU...WISE JEN...
WHAT HAPPENED?
THE SKEKSIS. THE CHAMBERLAIN.
GARTHIM ARE...NN...H-HIS NOW.
SHOULD NEVER HAVE USED... WEAPONS OF OUR ENEMIES. FEAR MADE US BLIND.
F-FEAR OF THE SKEKSIS...
...FEAR OF THE DARK CRYSTAL.
REST, COMMANDER. WE'LL GET YOU OUT OF--
NO. BEYOND EVEN...YOUR HELP.
OTHERS AT CRYSTAL CASTLE...NEED YOU. LADY KIRA NEEDS YOU.
EVEN BROKEN...
...THE WILL OF THE CRYSTAL... IS WITH YOU.

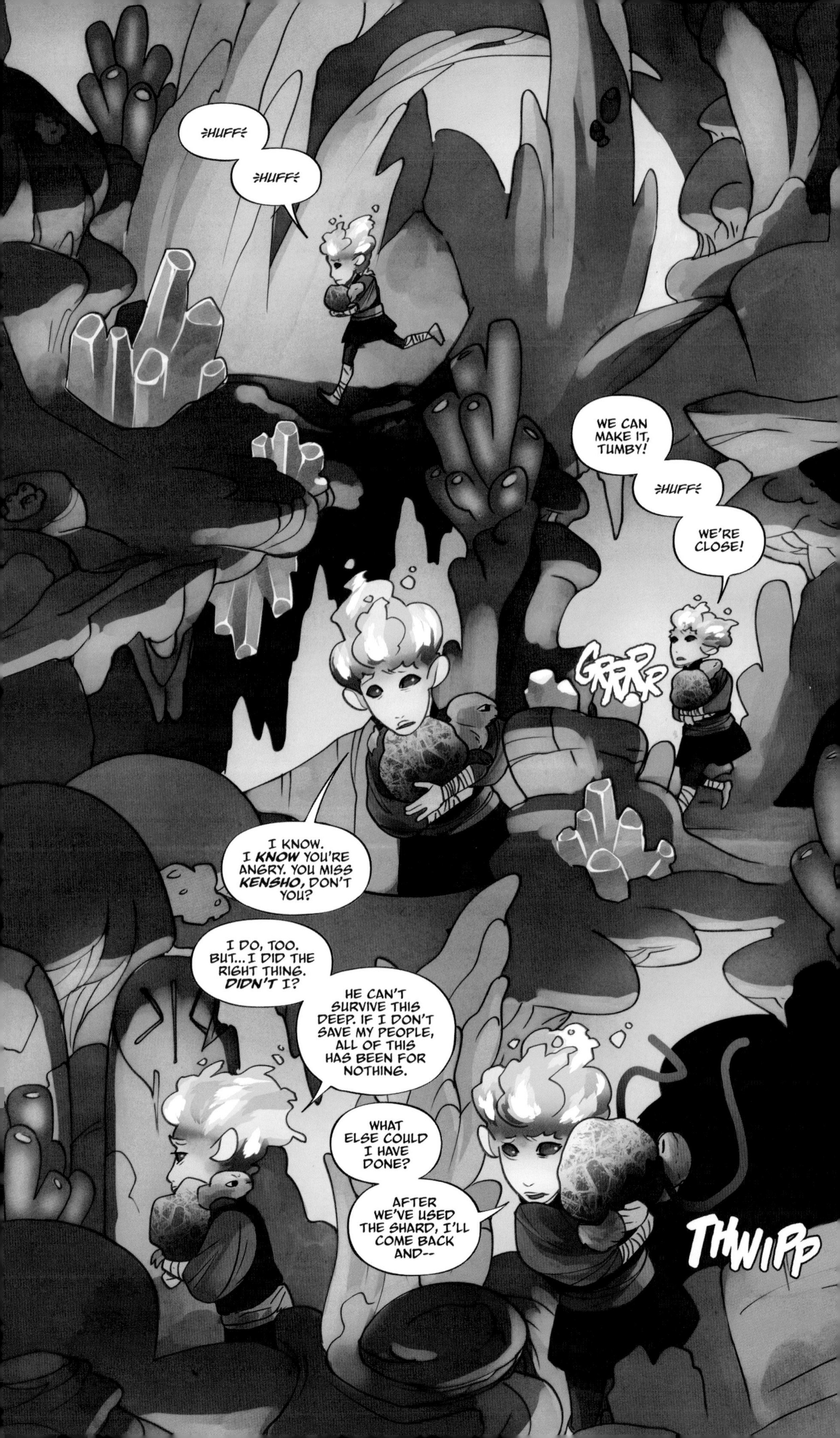

HUFF
HUFF
WE CAN MAKE IT, TUMBY!
HUFF
WE'RE CLOSE!
GRRRR
I KNOW. I **KNOW** YOU'RE ANGRY. YOU MISS **KENSHO,** DON'T YOU?
I DO, TOO. BUT... I DID THE RIGHT THING. ***DIDN'T*** I?
HE CAN'T SURVIVE THIS DEEP. IF I DON'T SAVE MY PEOPLE, ALL OF THIS HAS BEEN FOR NOTHING.
WHAT ELSE COULD I HAVE DONE?
AFTER WE'VE USED THE SHARD, I'LL COME BACK AND--
THWIPP

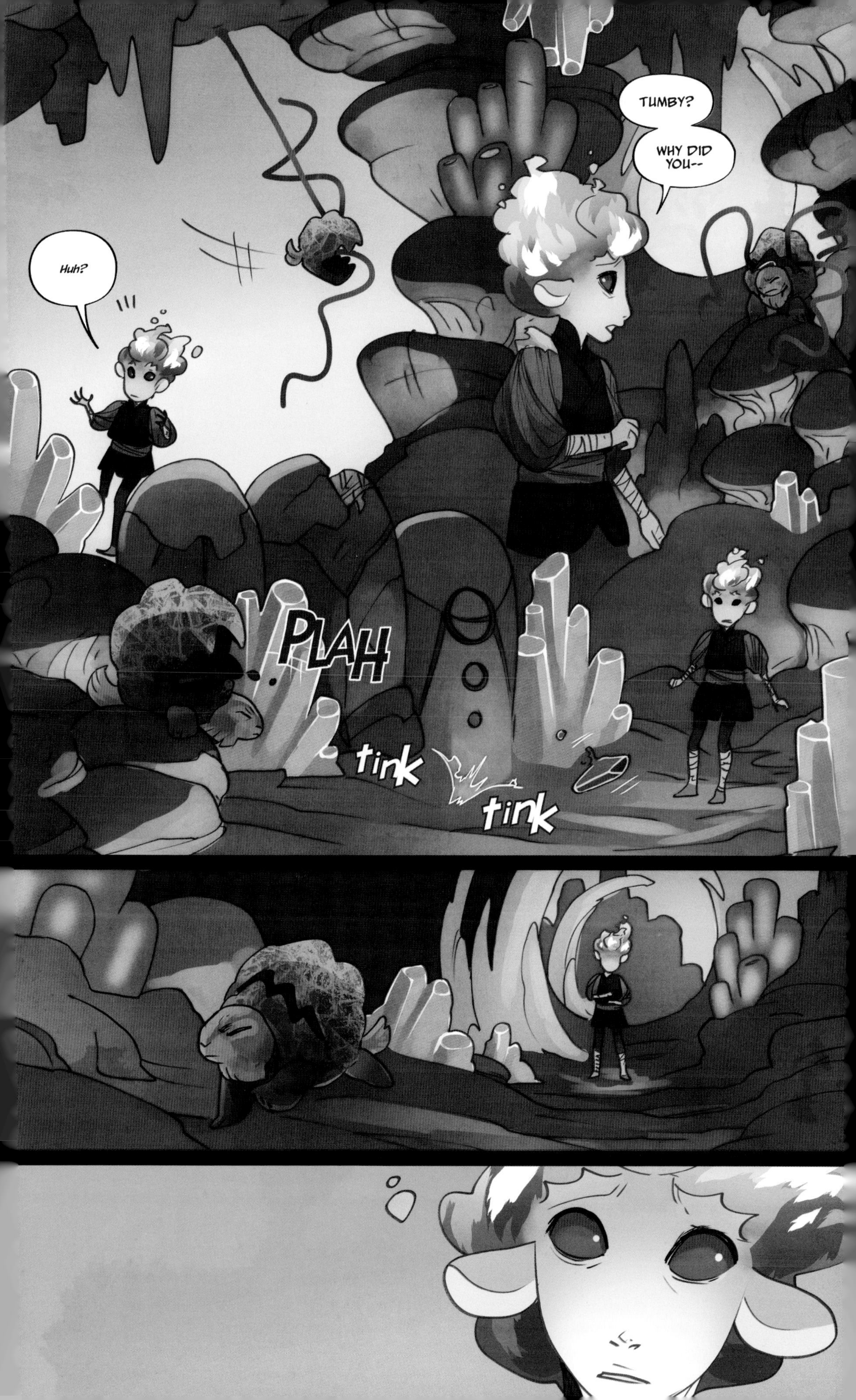
TUMBY?
WHY DID YOU--
Huh?
PLAH
tink
tink

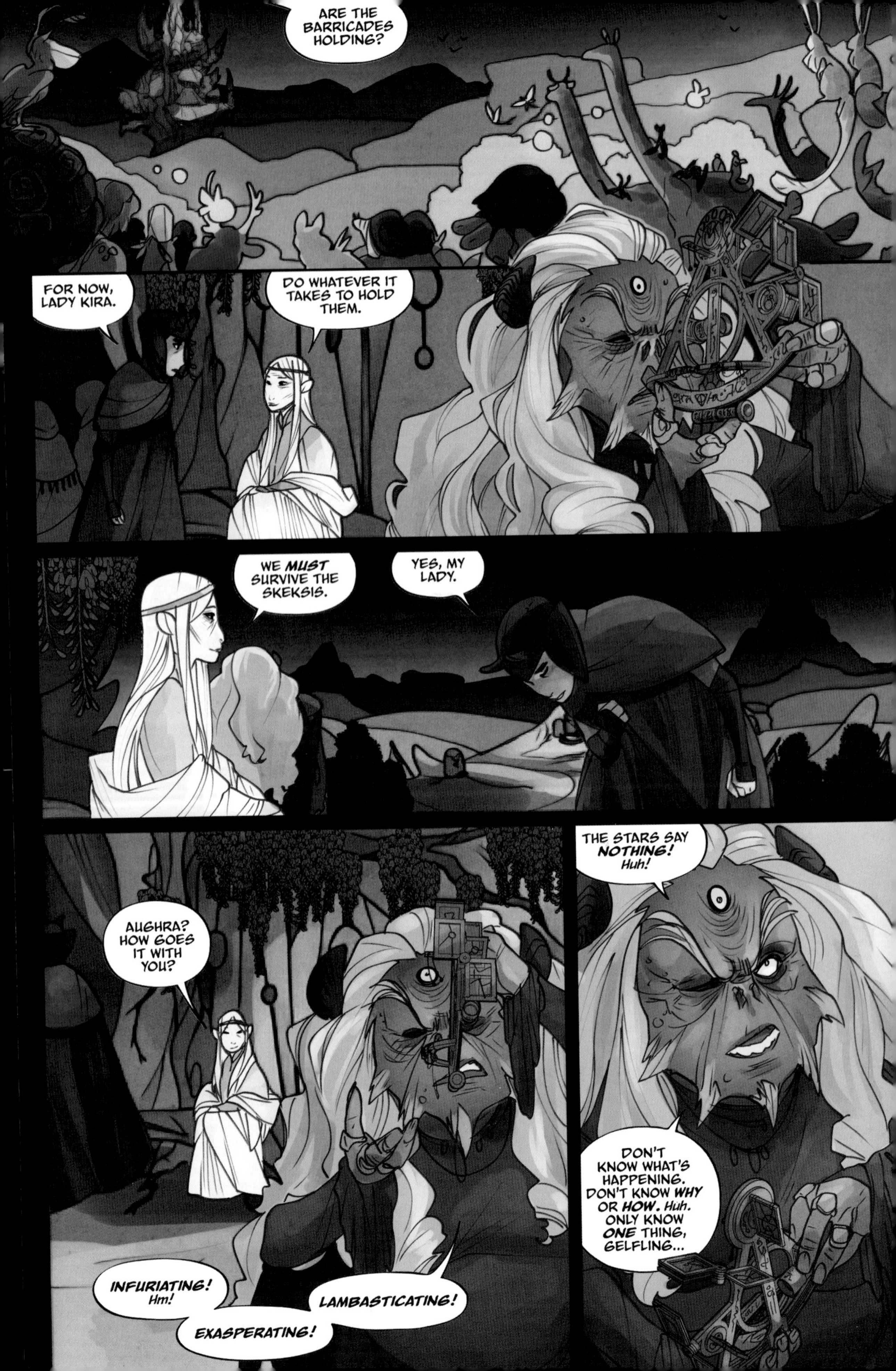
ARE THE BARRICADES HOLDING?
FOR NOW, LADY KIRA.
DO WHATEVER IT TAKES TO HOLD THEM.
WE *MUST* SURVIVE THE SKEKSIS.
YES, MY LADY.
AUGHRA? HOW GOES IT WITH YOU?
INFURIATING! *Hm!*
EXASPERATING!
LAMBASTICATING!
THE STARS SAY *NOTHING!* *Huh!*
DON'T KNOW WHAT'S HAPPENING. DON'T KNOW *WHY* OR *HOW*. *Huh.* ONLY KNOW *ONE* THING, GELFLING...

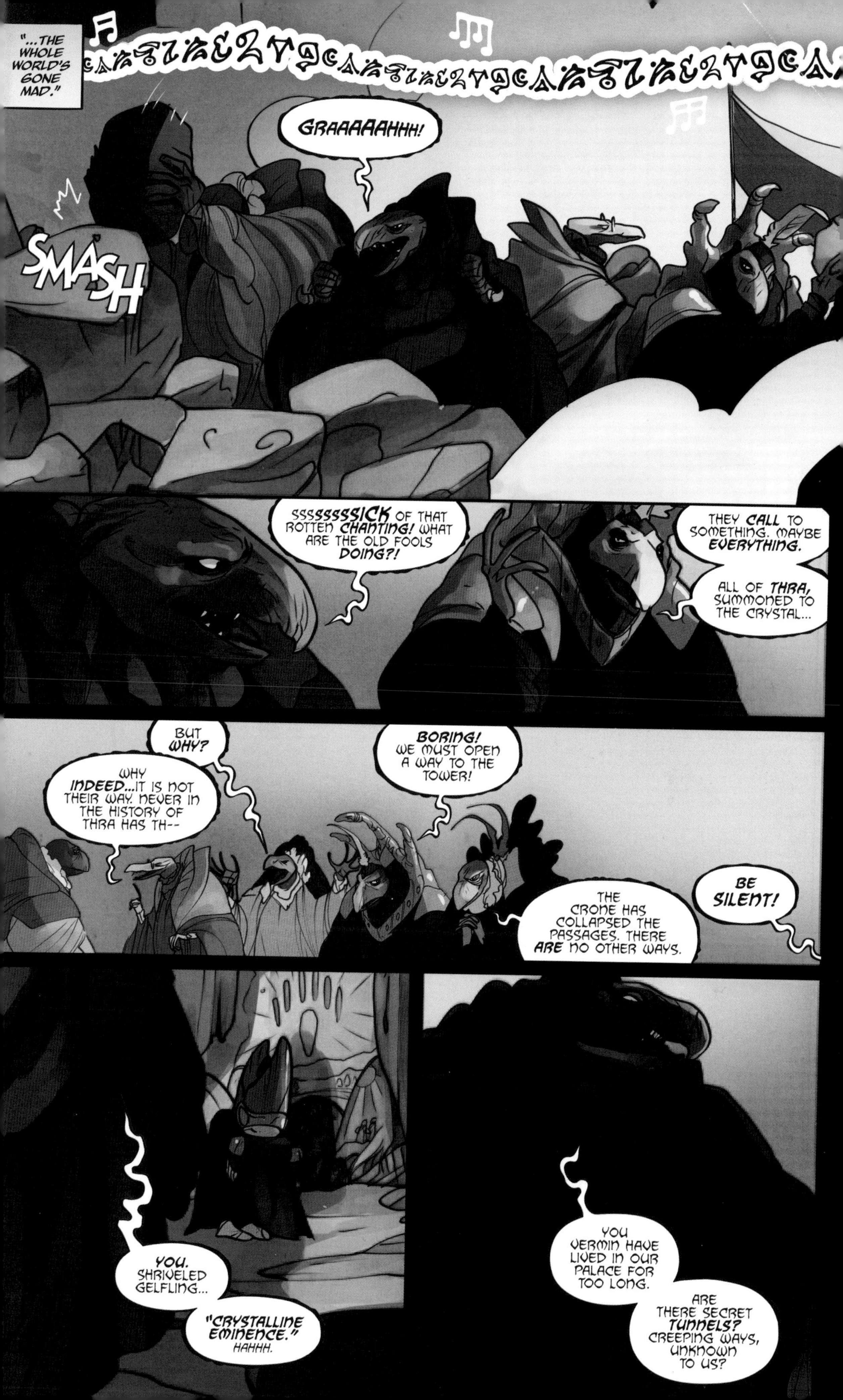
"...THE WHOLE WORLD'S GONE MAD."
GRAAAAAHHH!
SMASH
SSSSSSSSICK OF THAT ROTTEN CHANTING! WHAT ARE THE OLD FOOLS DOING?!
THEY CALL TO SOMETHING. MAYBE EVERYTHING.
ALL OF THRA, SUMMONED TO THE CRYSTAL...
BUT WHY?
WHY INDEED...IT IS NOT THEIR WAY. NEVER IN THE HISTORY OF THRA HAS TH--
BORING! WE MUST OPEN A WAY TO THE TOWER!
THE CRONE HAS COLLAPSED THE PASSAGES. THERE ARE NO OTHER WAYS.
BE SILENT!
YOU. SHRIVELED GELFLING...
"CRYSTALLINE EMINENCE." HAHHH.
YOU VERMIN HAVE LIVED IN OUR PALACE FOR TOO LONG.
ARE THERE SECRET TUNNELS? CREEPING WAYS, UNKNOWN TO US?

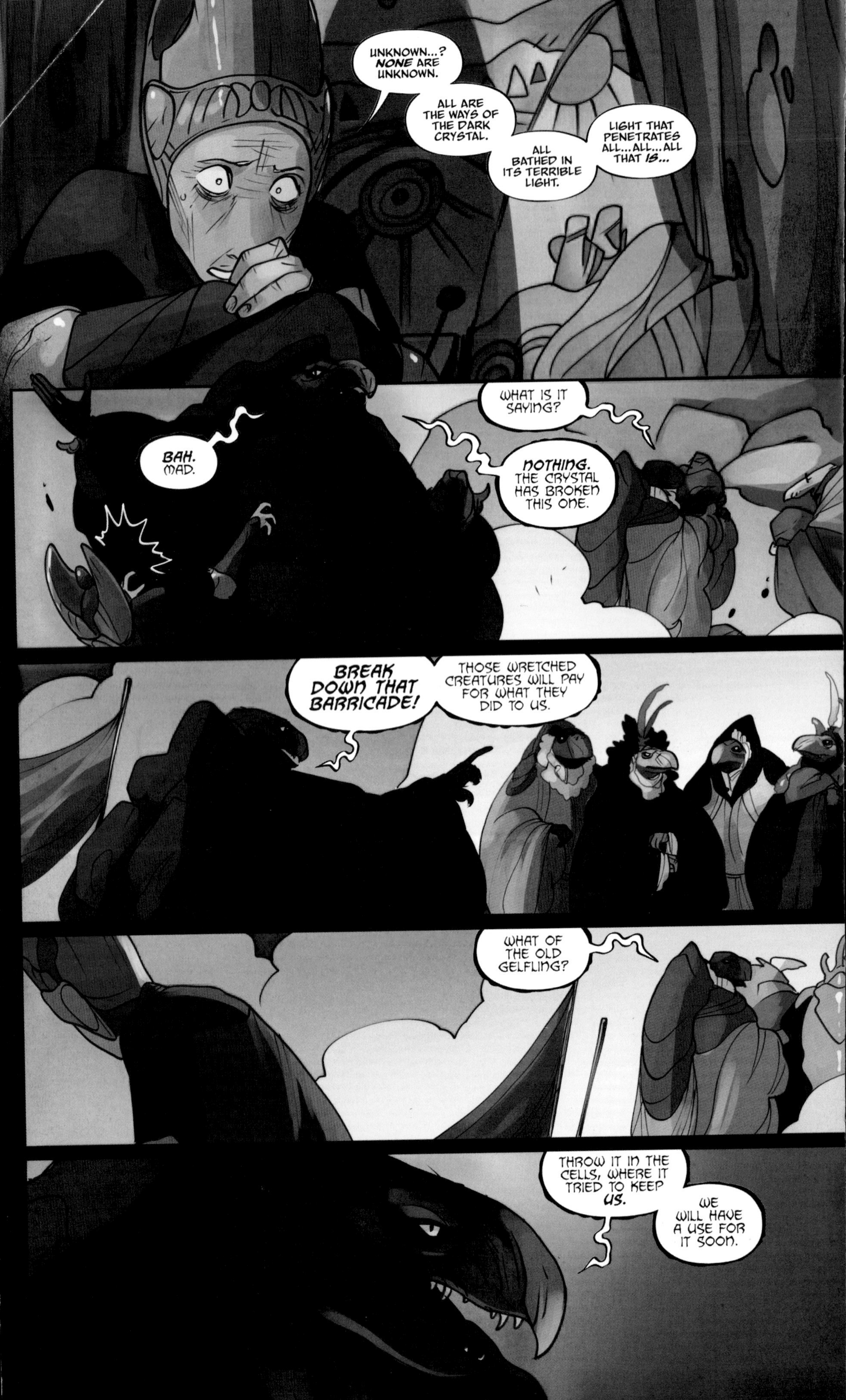
UNKNOWN...? NONE ARE UNKNOWN.
ALL ARE THE WAYS OF THE DARK CRYSTAL.
ALL BATHED IN ITS TERRIBLE LIGHT.
LIGHT THAT PENETRATES ALL... ALL... ALL THAT IS...
WHAT IS IT SAYING?
BAH. MAD.
NOTHING. THE CRYSTAL HAS BROKEN THIS ONE.
BREAK DOWN THAT BARRICADE!
THOSE WRETCHED CREATURES WILL PAY FOR WHAT THEY DID TO US.
WHAT OF THE OLD GELFLING?
THROW IT IN THE CELLS, WHERE IT TRIED TO KEEP US.
WE WILL HAVE A USE FOR IT SOON.

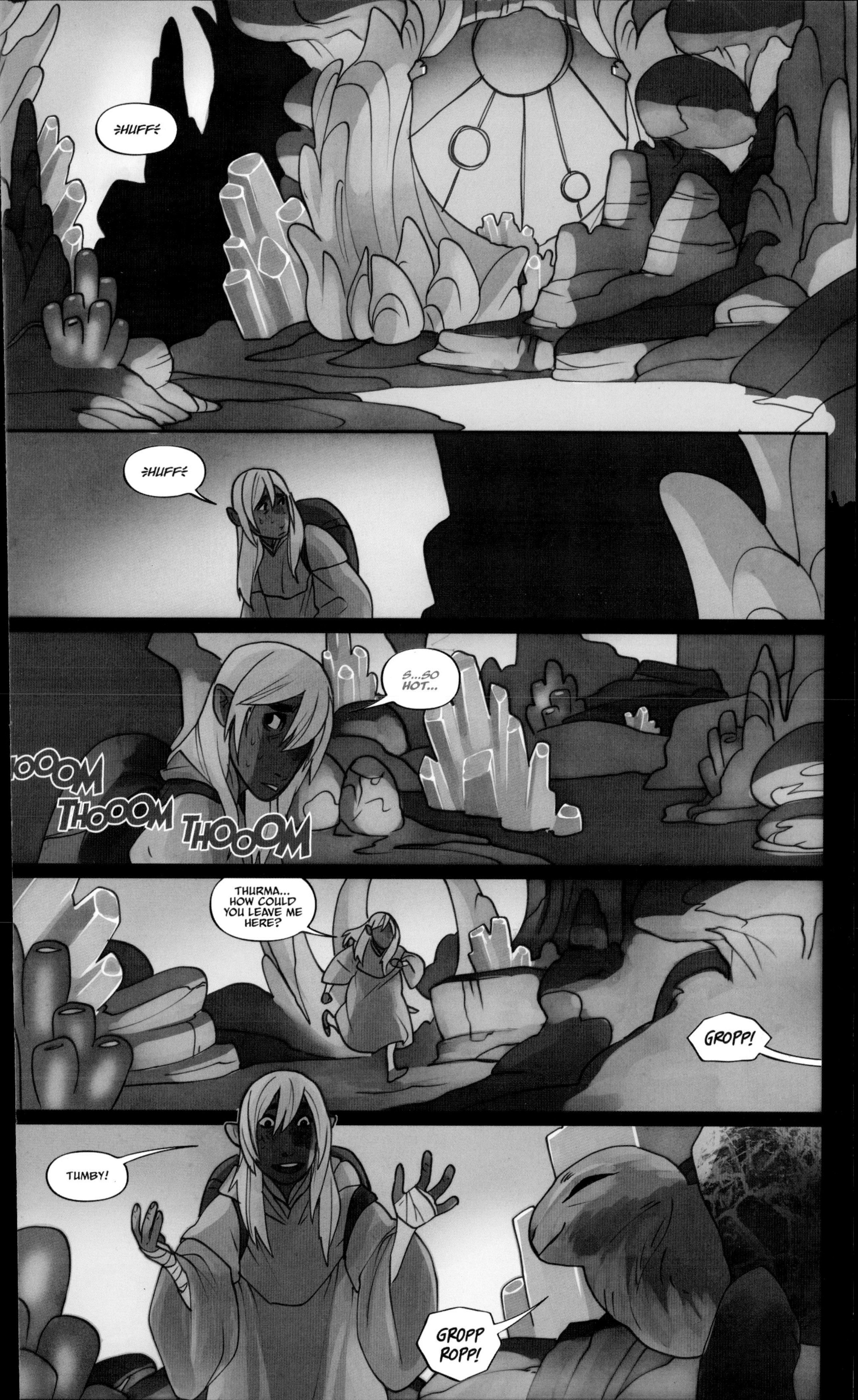

HUFF
HUFF
S...SO HOT...
THOOOM THOOOM THOOOM
THURMA... HOW COULD YOU LEAVE ME HERE?
GROPP!
TUMBY!
GROPP ROPP!

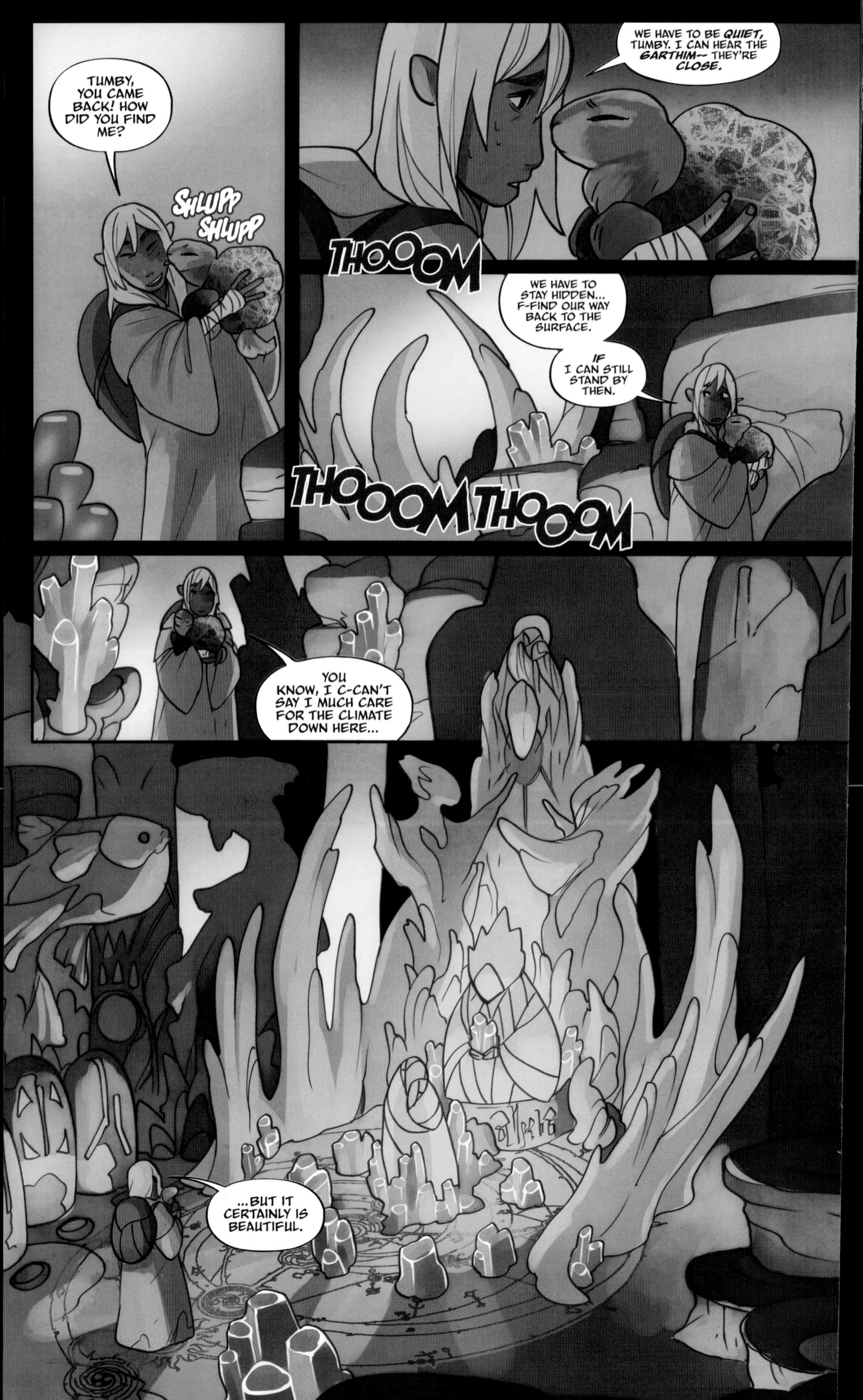
TUMBY, YOU CAME BACK! HOW DID YOU FIND ME?
SHLUPP SHLUPP
WE HAVE TO BE QUIET, TUMBY. I CAN HEAR THE GARTHIM-- THEY'RE CLOSE.
THOOOM
WE HAVE TO STAY HIDDEN... F-FIND OUR WAY BACK TO THE SURFACE.
IF I CAN STILL STAND BY THEN.
THOOOM THOOOM
YOU KNOW, I C-CAN'T SAY I MUCH CARE FOR THE CLIMATE DOWN HERE...
...BUT IT CERTAINLY IS BEAUTIFUL.

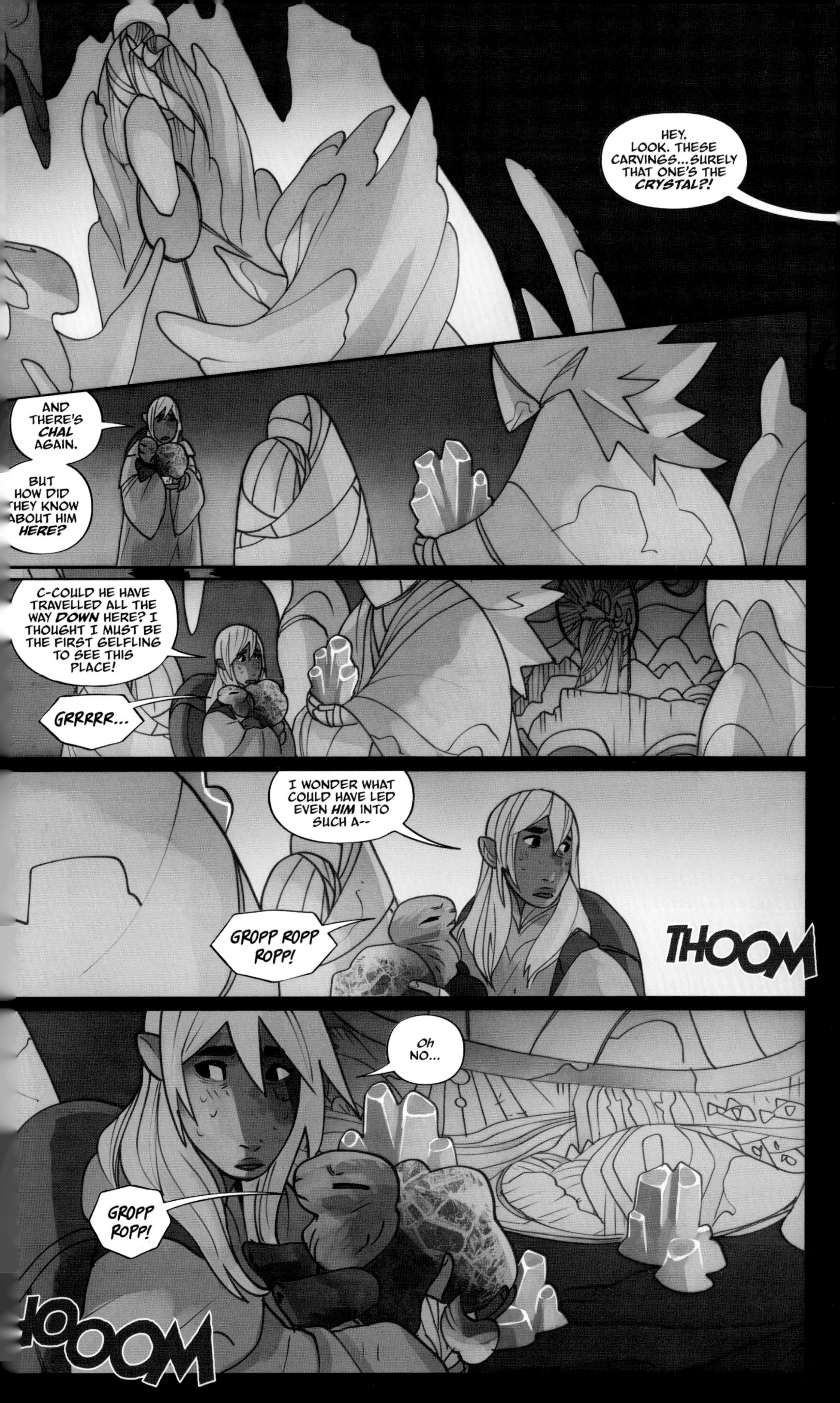
HEY. LOOK. THESE CARVINGS...SURELY THAT ONE'S THE CRYSTAL?!
AND THERE'S CHAL AGAIN.
BUT HOW DID THEY KNOW ABOUT HIM HERE?
C-COULD HE HAVE TRAVELLED ALL THE WAY DOWN HERE? I THOUGHT I MUST BE THE FIRST GELFLING TO SEE THIS PLACE!
GRRRRR...
I WONDER WHAT COULD HAVE LED EVEN HIM INTO SUCH A--
GROPP ROPP ROPP!
THOOM
OH NO...
GROPP ROPP!
OOOM

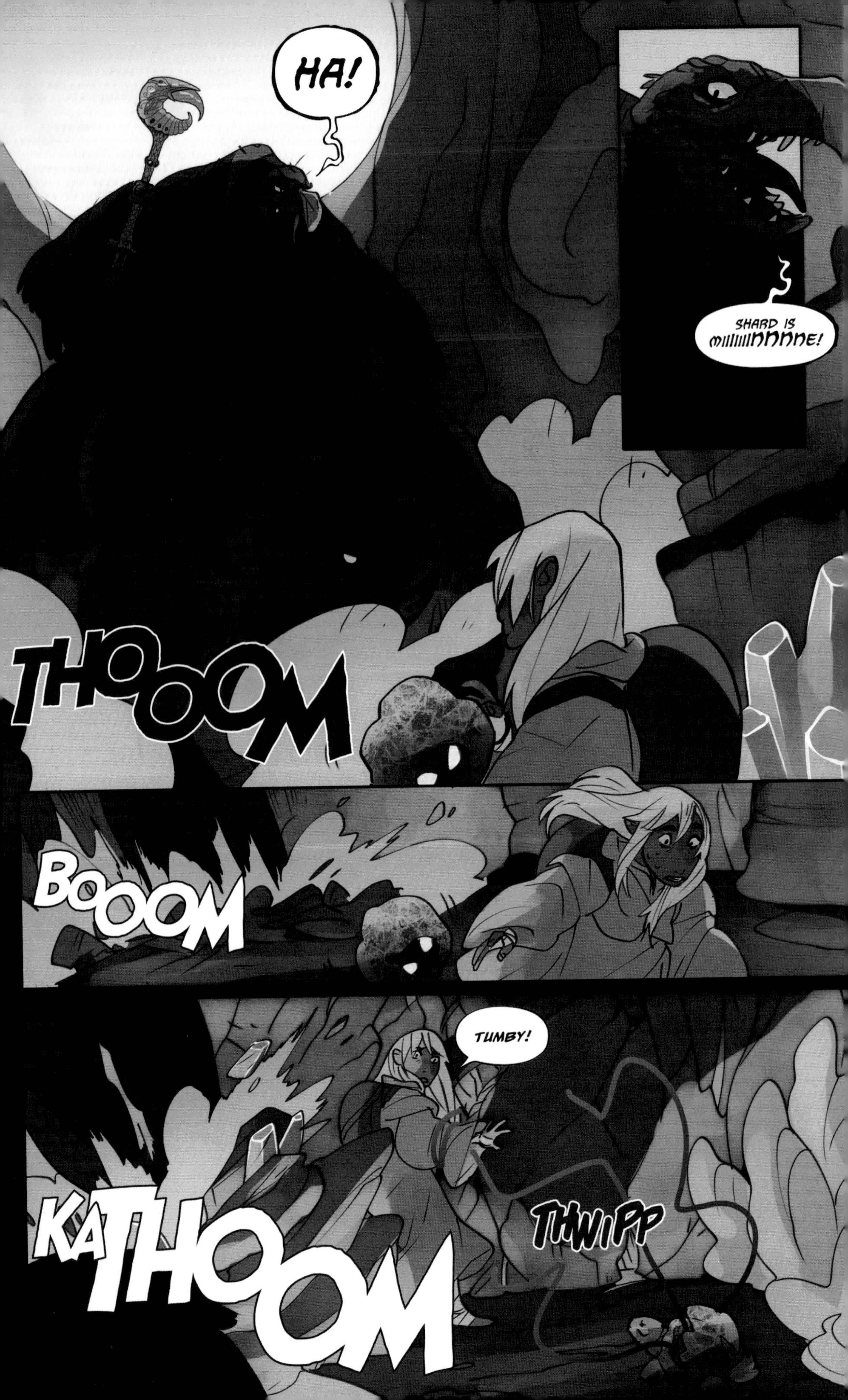
HA!
SHARD IS MIIIIIINNNNE!
THOOOM
BOOOOM
TUMBY!
KATHOOOM
THWIPP

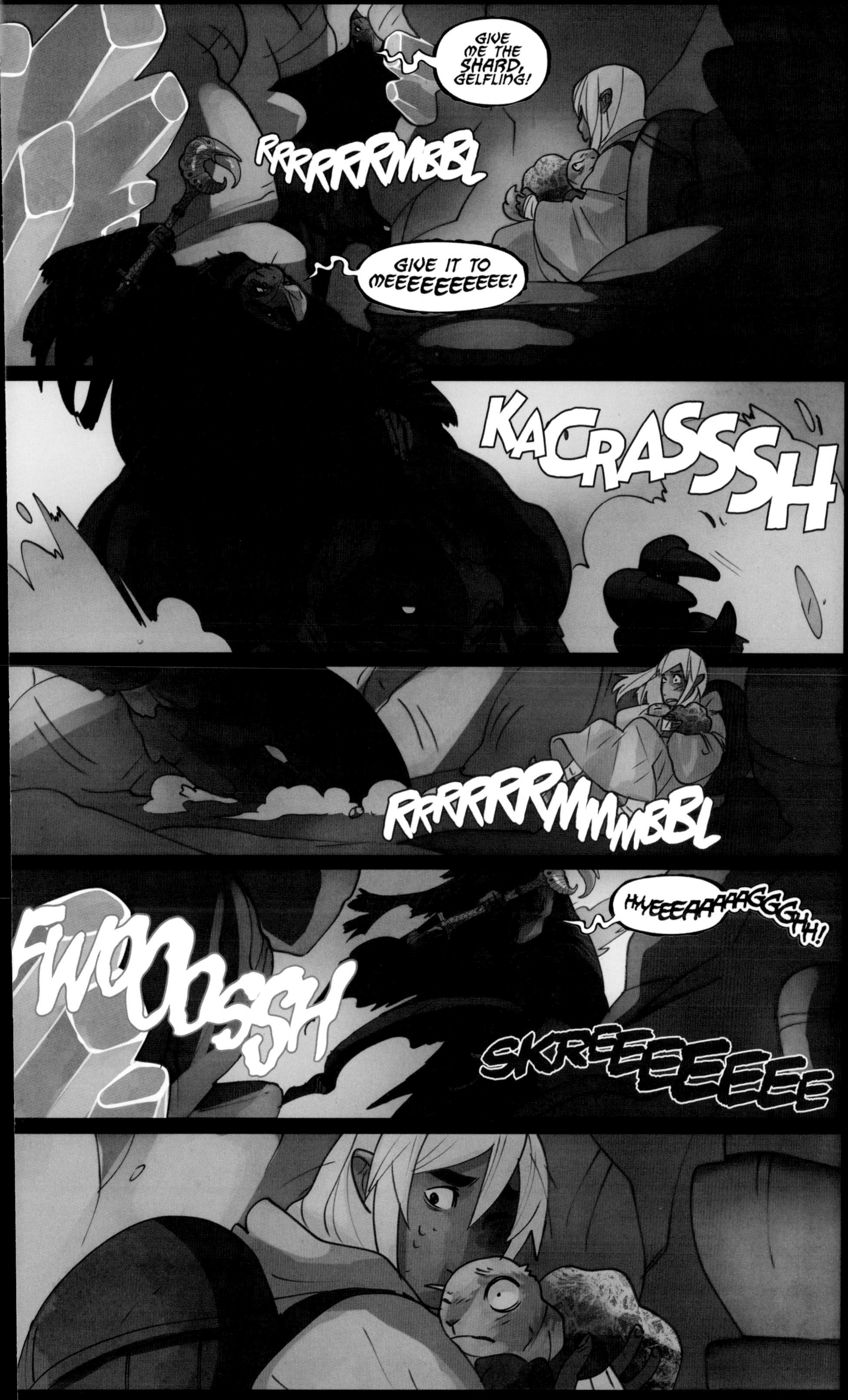
GIVE ME THE SHARD, GELFLING!
RRRRRRRMBBL
GIVE IT TO MEEEEEEEEEEE!
KACRASSSSH
RRRRRRRMMMBBL
FWOOOSSH
HYEEEAAAAAGGGHH!
SKREEEEEEEEE

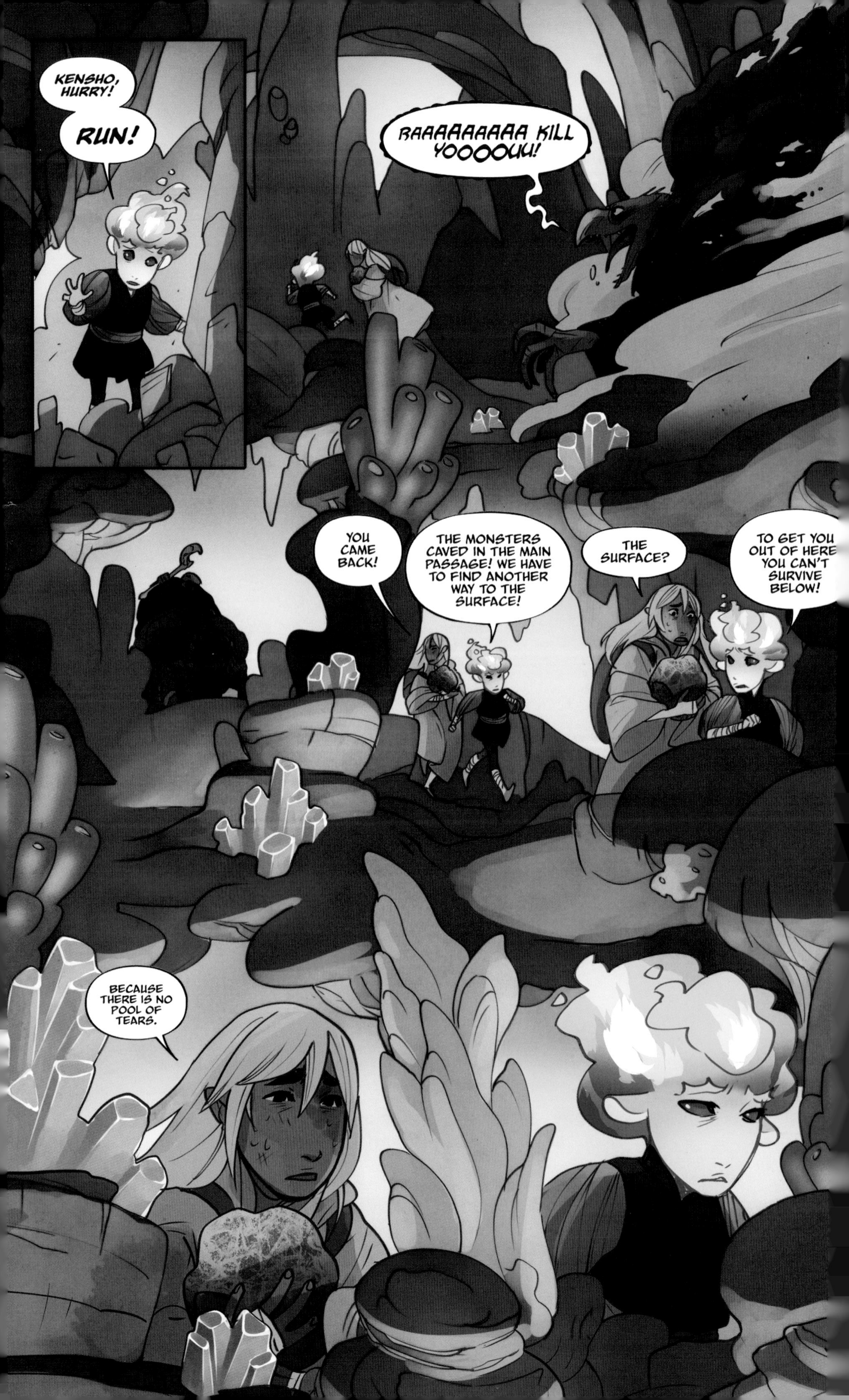
KENSHO, HURRY!
RUN!
BAAAAAAAAA KILL YOOOOUU!
YOU CAME BACK!
THE MONSTERS CAVED IN THE MAIN PASSAGE! WE HAVE TO FIND ANOTHER WAY TO THE SURFACE!
THE SURFACE?
TO GET YOU OUT OF HERE YOU CAN'T SURVIVE BELOW!
BECAUSE THERE IS NO POOL OF TEARS.

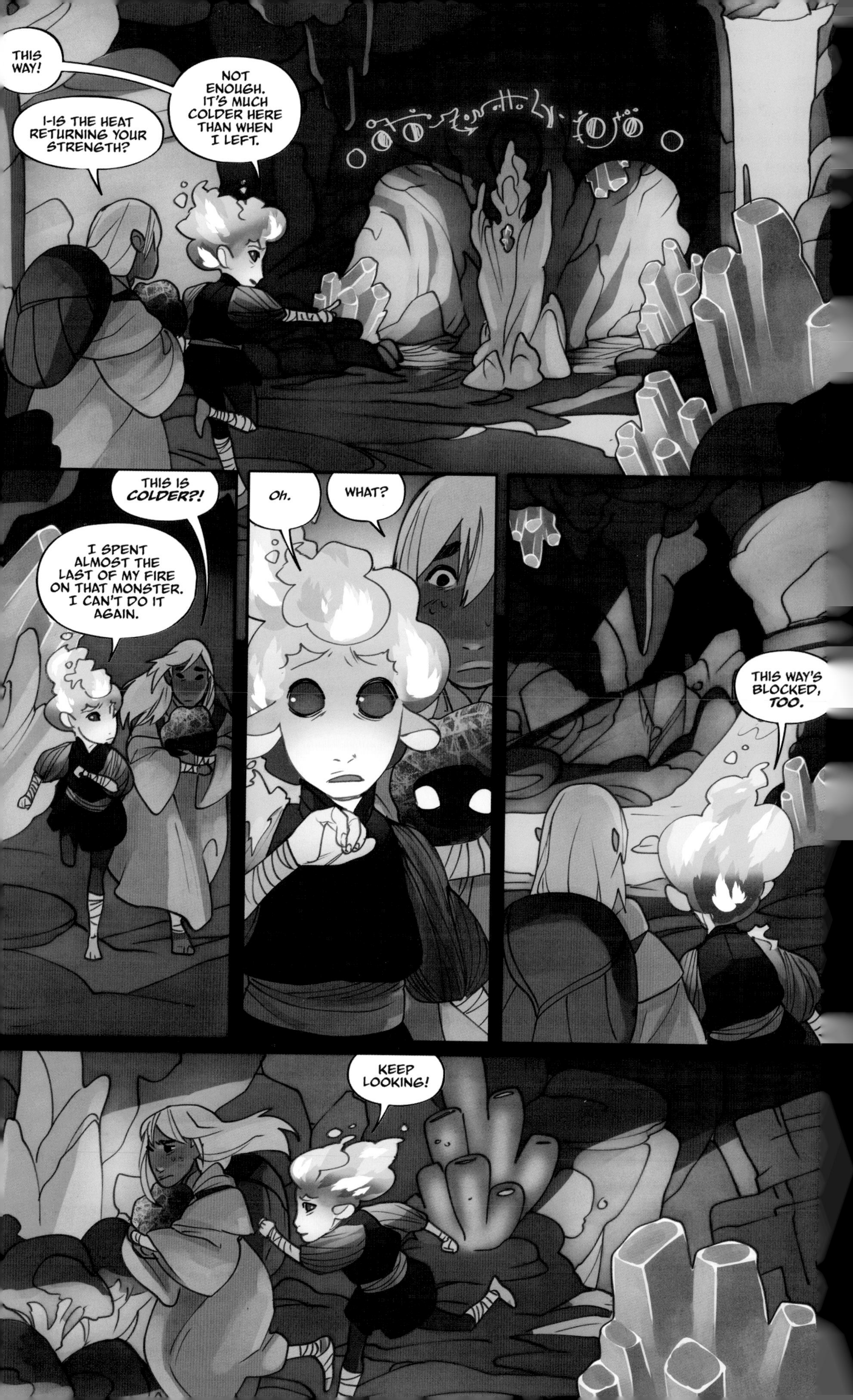
THIS WAY!
I-IS THE HEAT RETURNING YOUR STRENGTH?
NOT ENOUGH. IT'S MUCH COLDER HERE THAN WHEN I LEFT.
THIS IS COLDER?!
I SPENT ALMOST THE LAST OF MY FIRE ON THAT MONSTER. I CAN'T DO IT AGAIN.
Oh.
WHAT?
THIS WAY'S BLOCKED, TOO.
KEEP LOOKING!

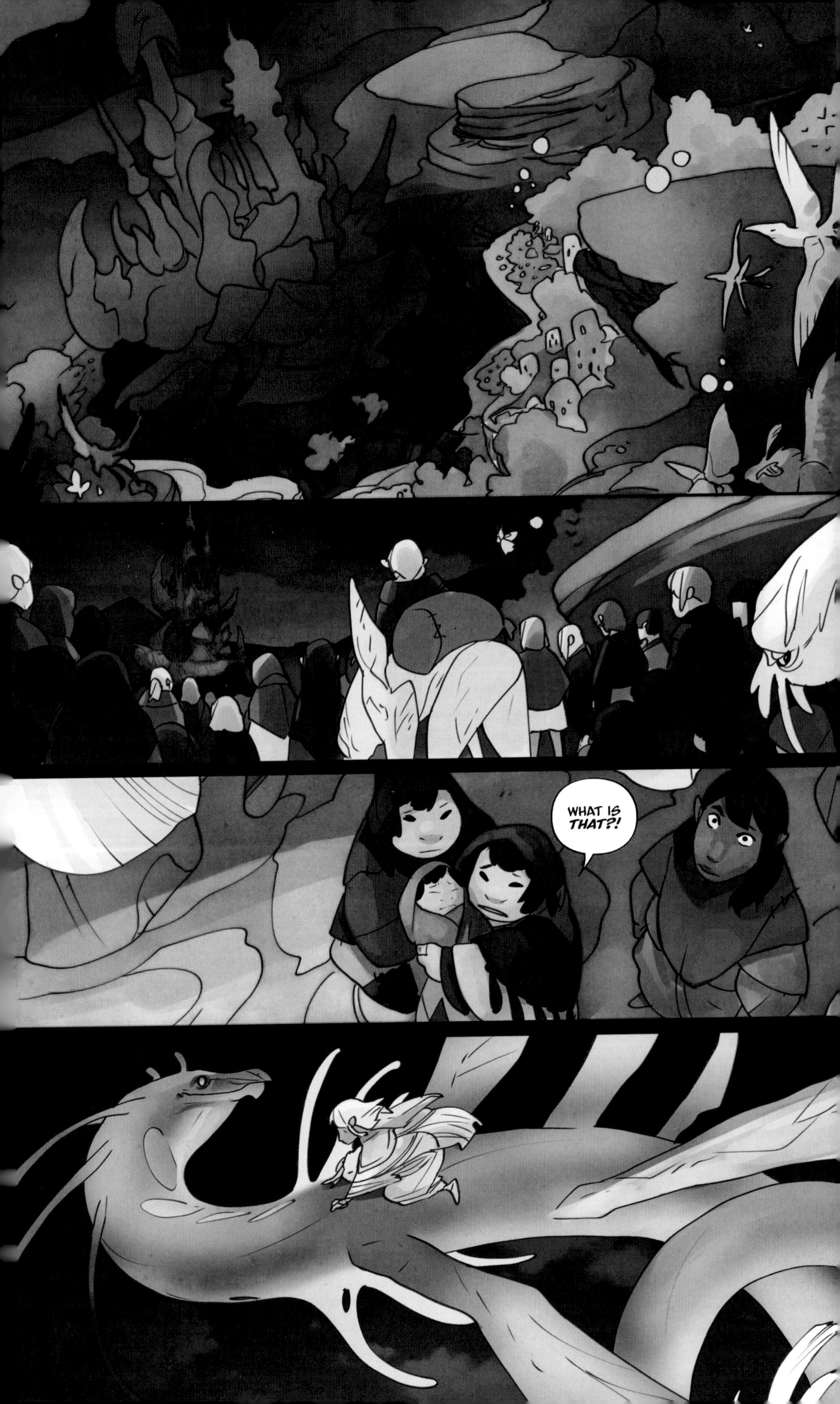
WHAT IS
THAT?!

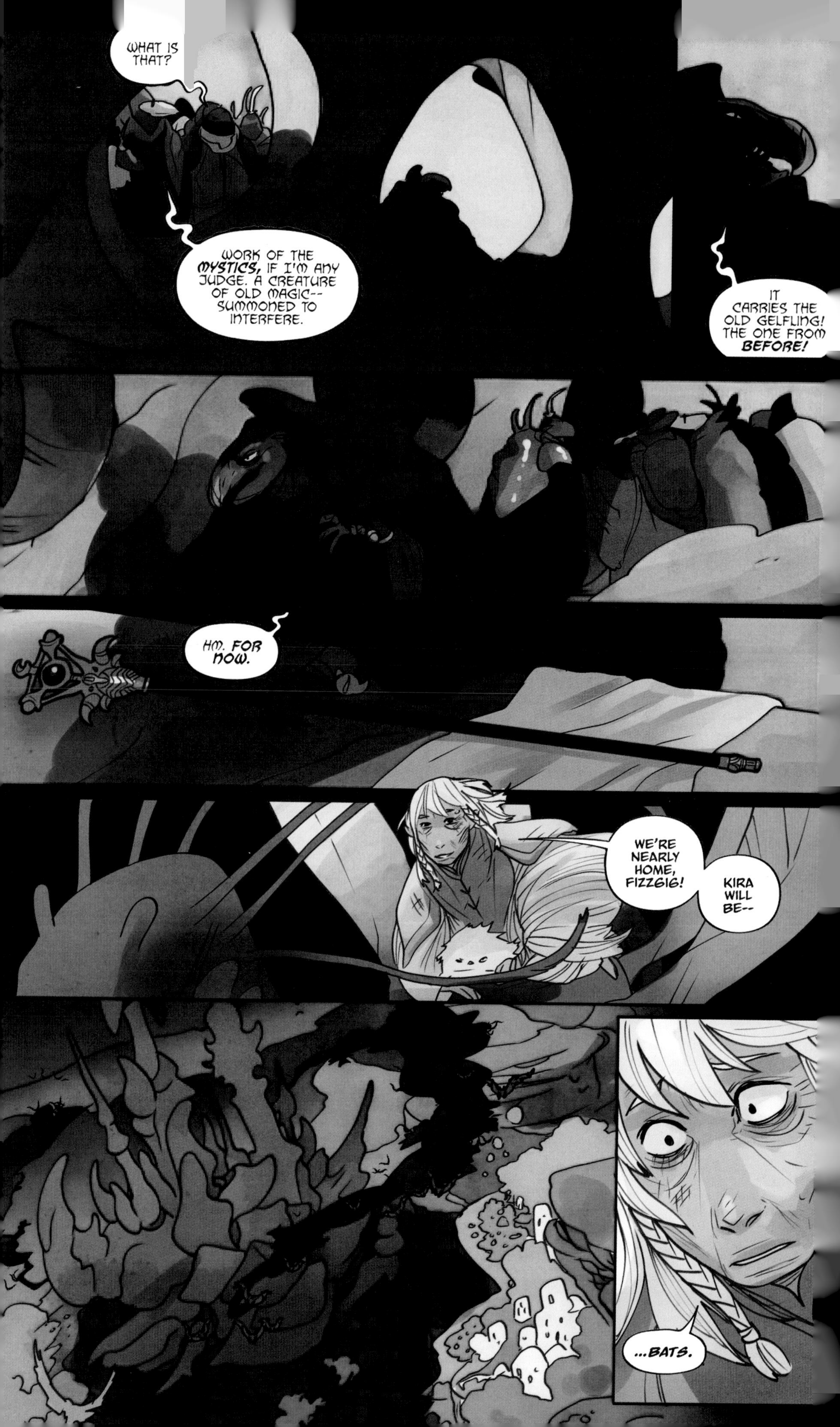
WHAT IS THAT?
WORK OF THE MYSTICS, IF I'M ANY JUDGE. A CREATURE OF OLD MAGIC--SUMMONED TO INTERFERE.
IT CARRIES THE OLD GELFLING! THE ONE FROM BEFORE!
HM. FOR NOW.
WE'RE NEARLY HOME, FIZZGIG!
KIRA WILL BE--
...BATS.

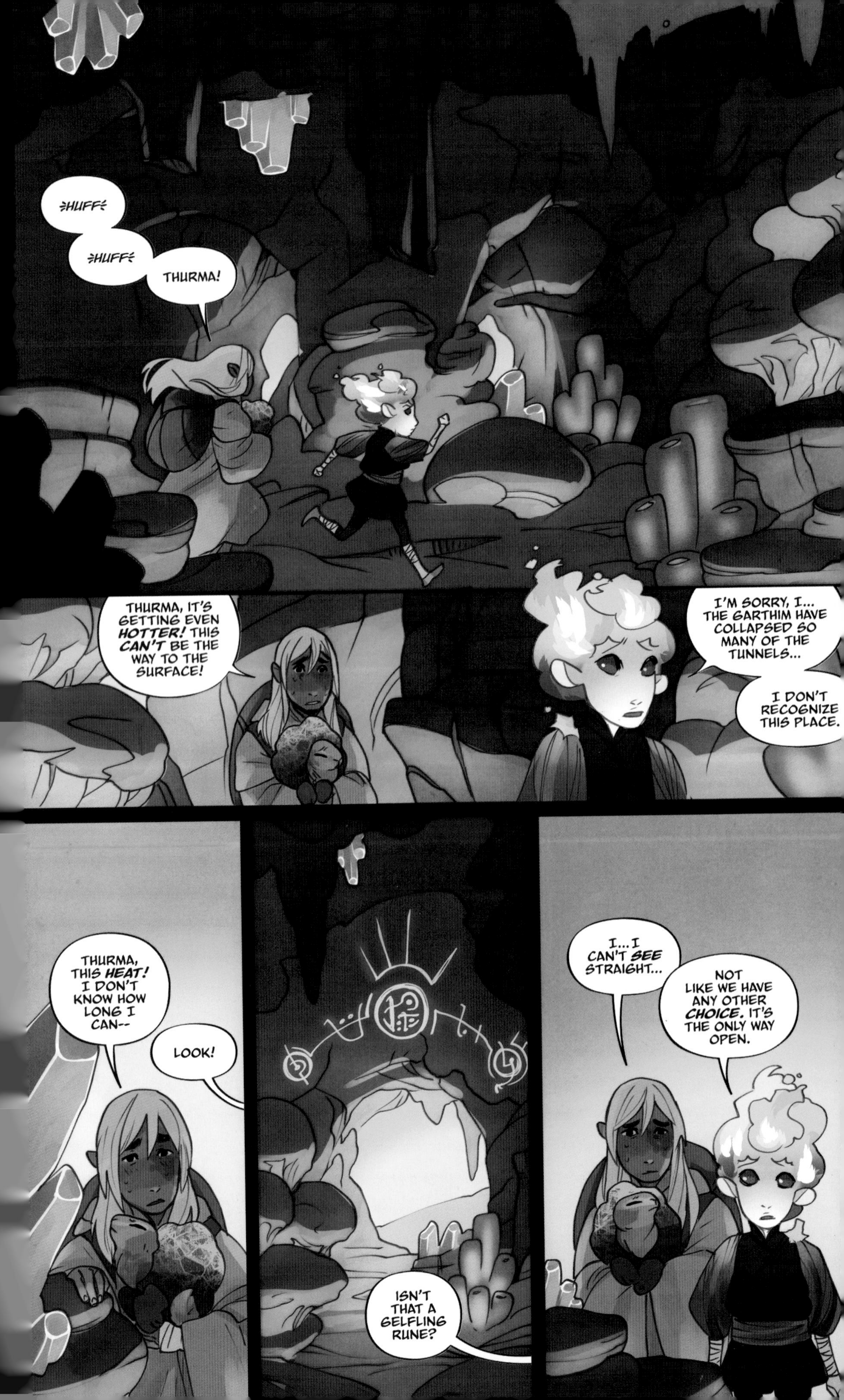

HUFF
HUFF
THURMA!
THURMA, IT'S GETTING EVEN HOTTER! THIS CAN'T BE THE WAY TO THE SURFACE!
I'M SORRY, I... THE GARTHIM HAVE COLLAPSED SO MANY OF THE TUNNELS...
I DON'T RECOGNIZE THIS PLACE.
THURMA, THIS HEAT! I DON'T KNOW HOW LONG I CAN--
LOOK!
ISN'T THAT A GELFLING RUNE?
I... I CAN'T SEE STRAIGHT...
NOT LIKE WE HAVE ANY OTHER CHOICE. IT'S THE ONLY WAY OPEN.

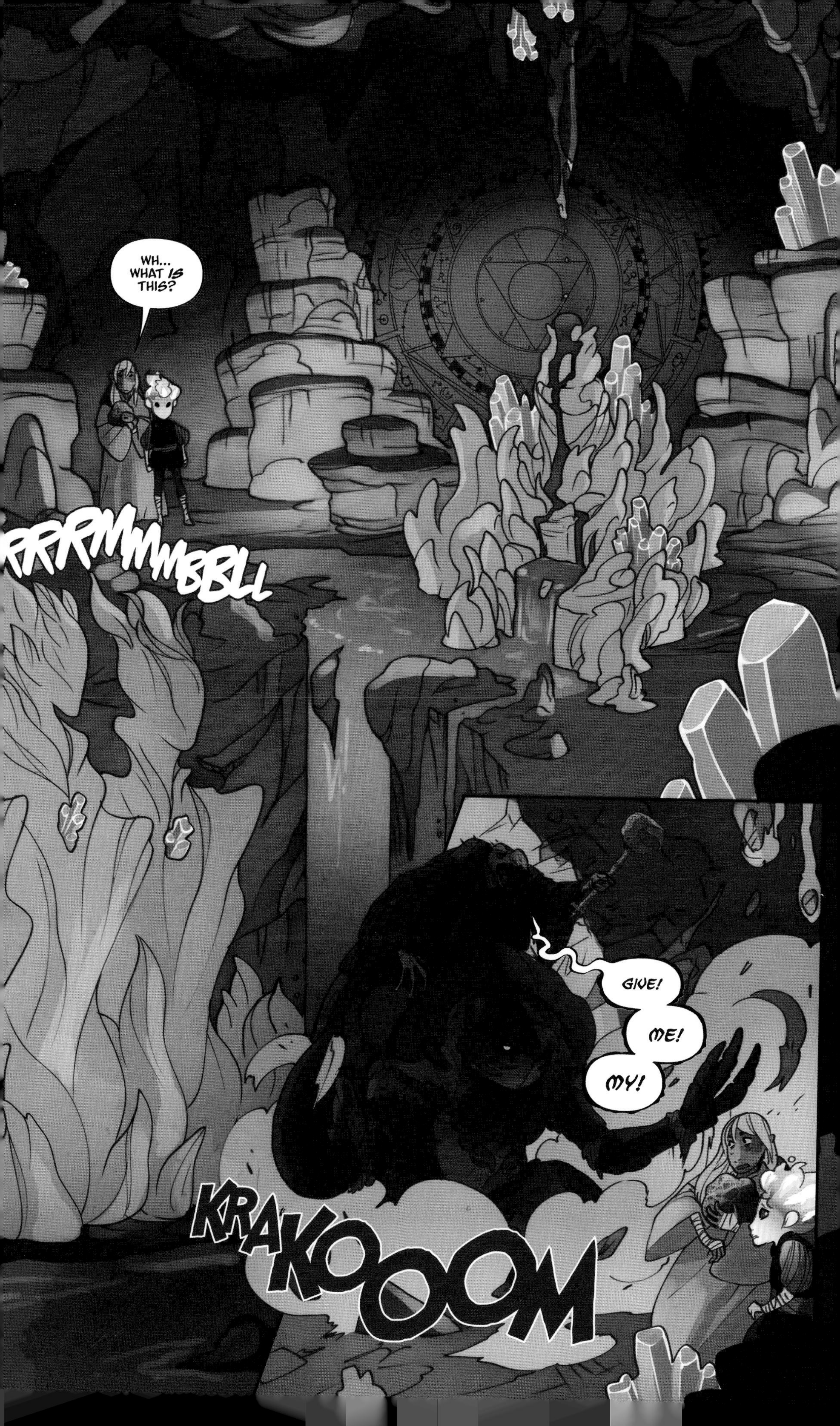
WH... WHAT *IS* THIS?
RRRMMMBBLL
GIVE!
ME!
MY!
KRAKOOOM

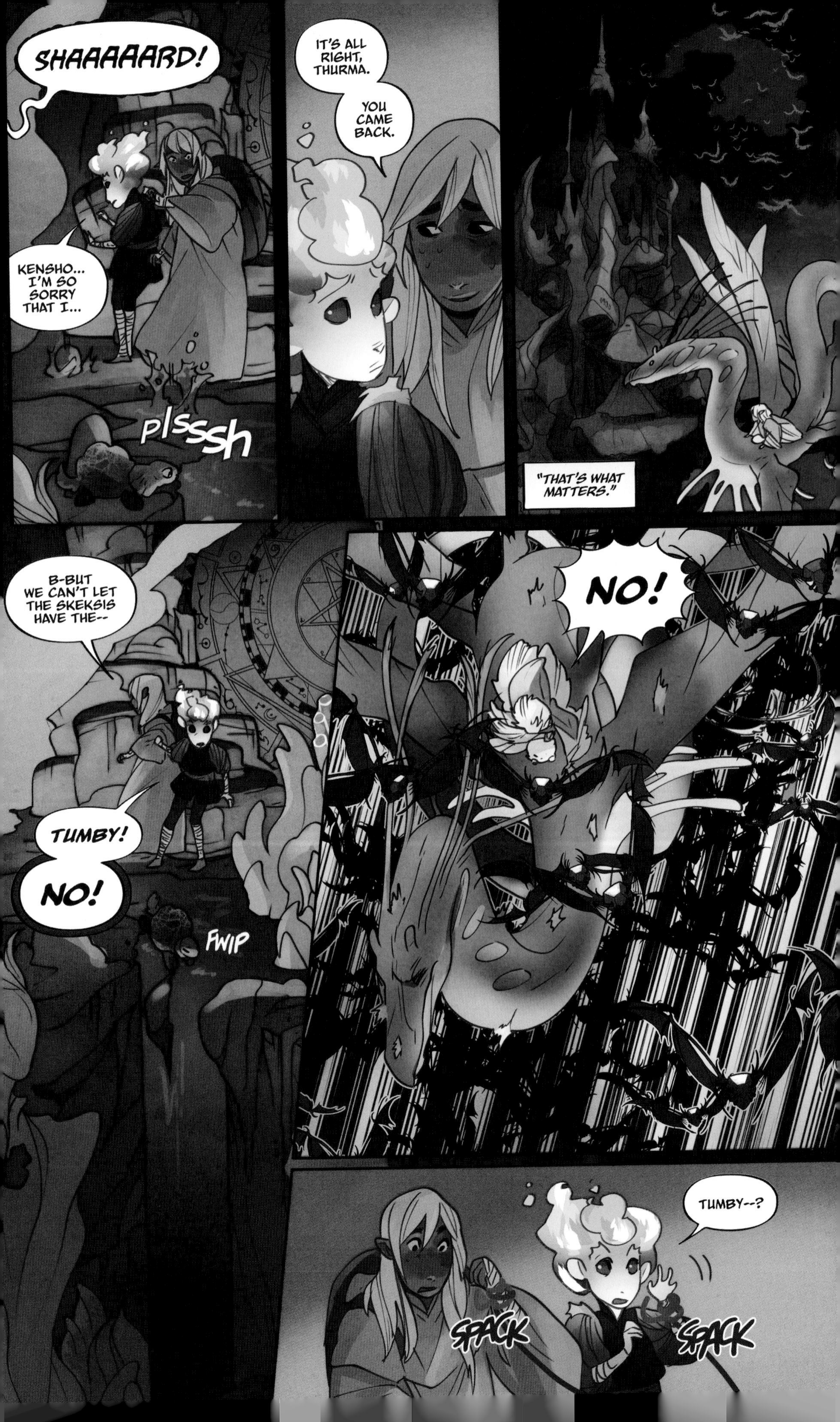
SHAAAAARD!
KENSHO... I'M SO SORRY THAT I...
plsssh
IT'S ALL RIGHT, THURMA.
YOU CAME BACK.
"THAT'S WHAT MATTERS."
B-BUT WE CAN'T LET THE SKEKSIS HAVE THE--
TUMBY!
NO!
FWIP
NO!
TUMBY--?
SPACK
SPACK

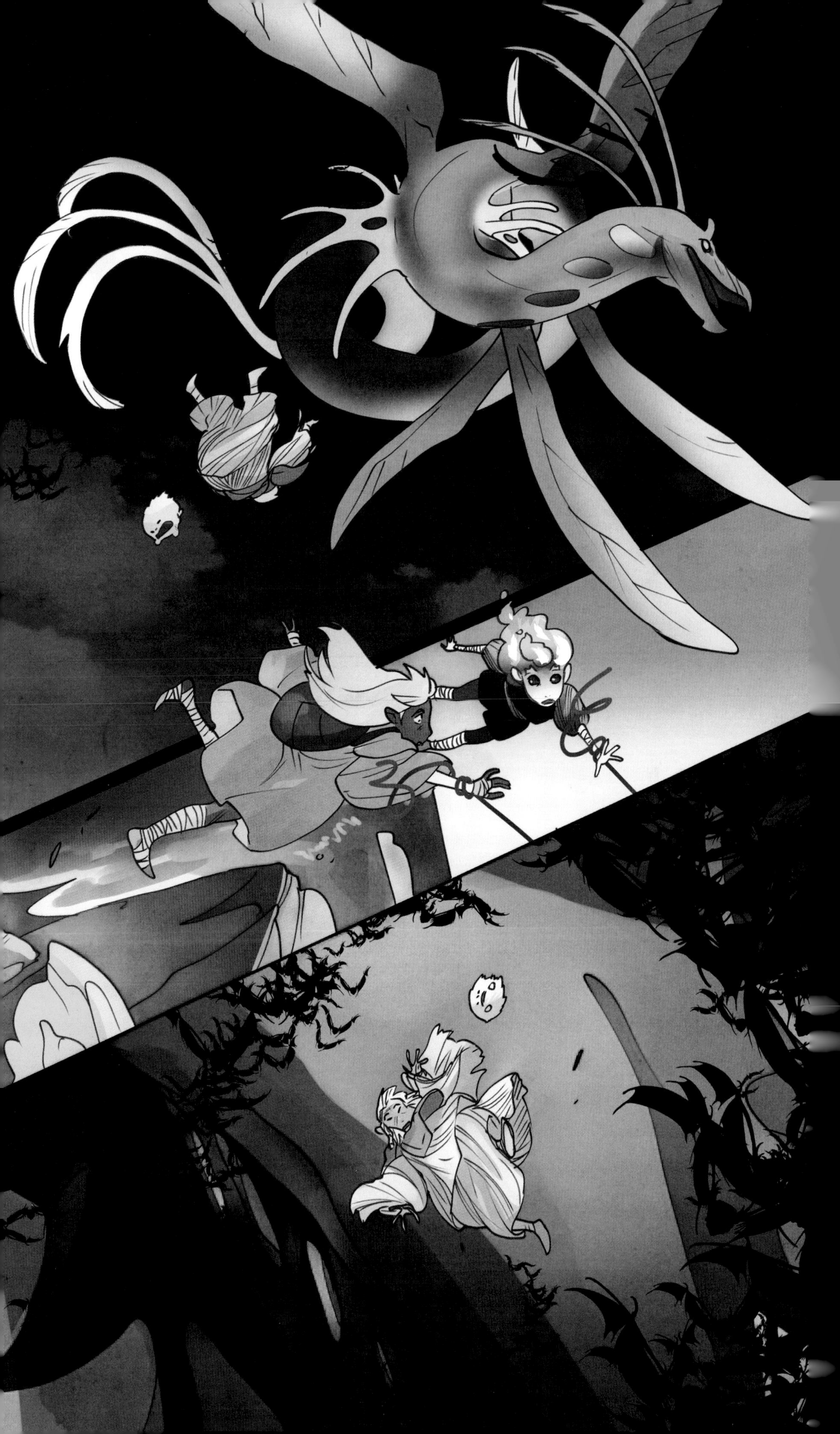

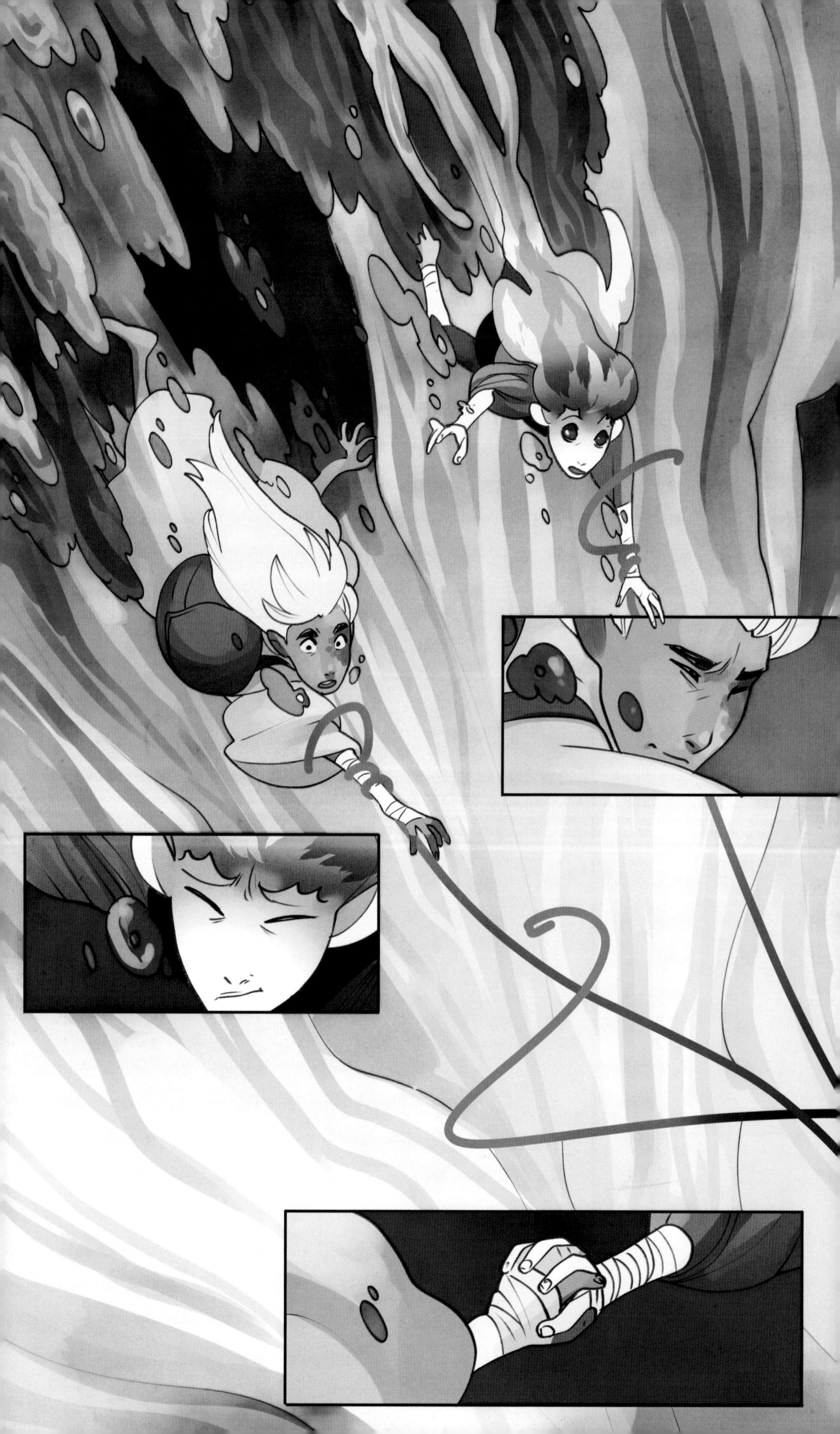

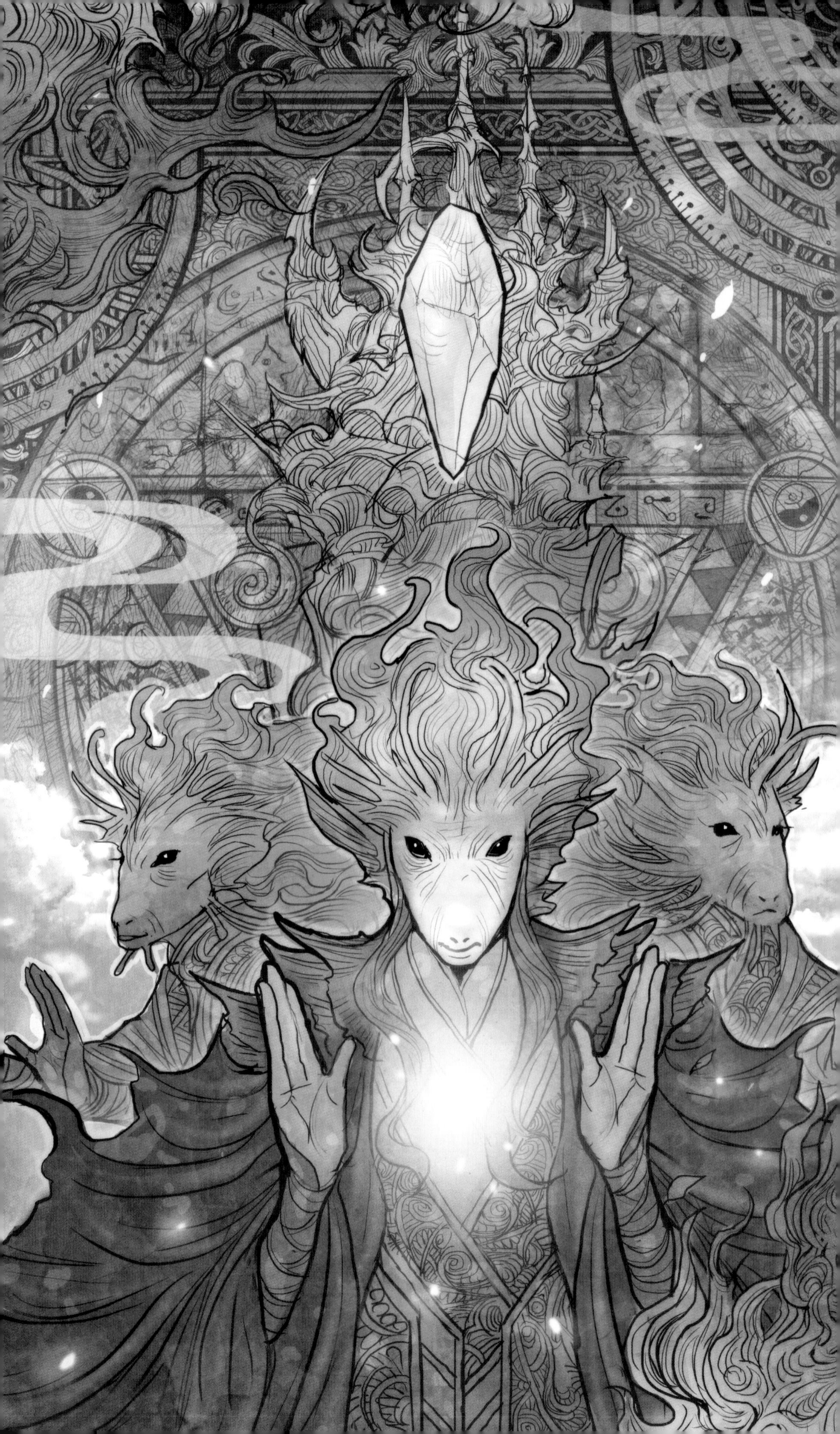

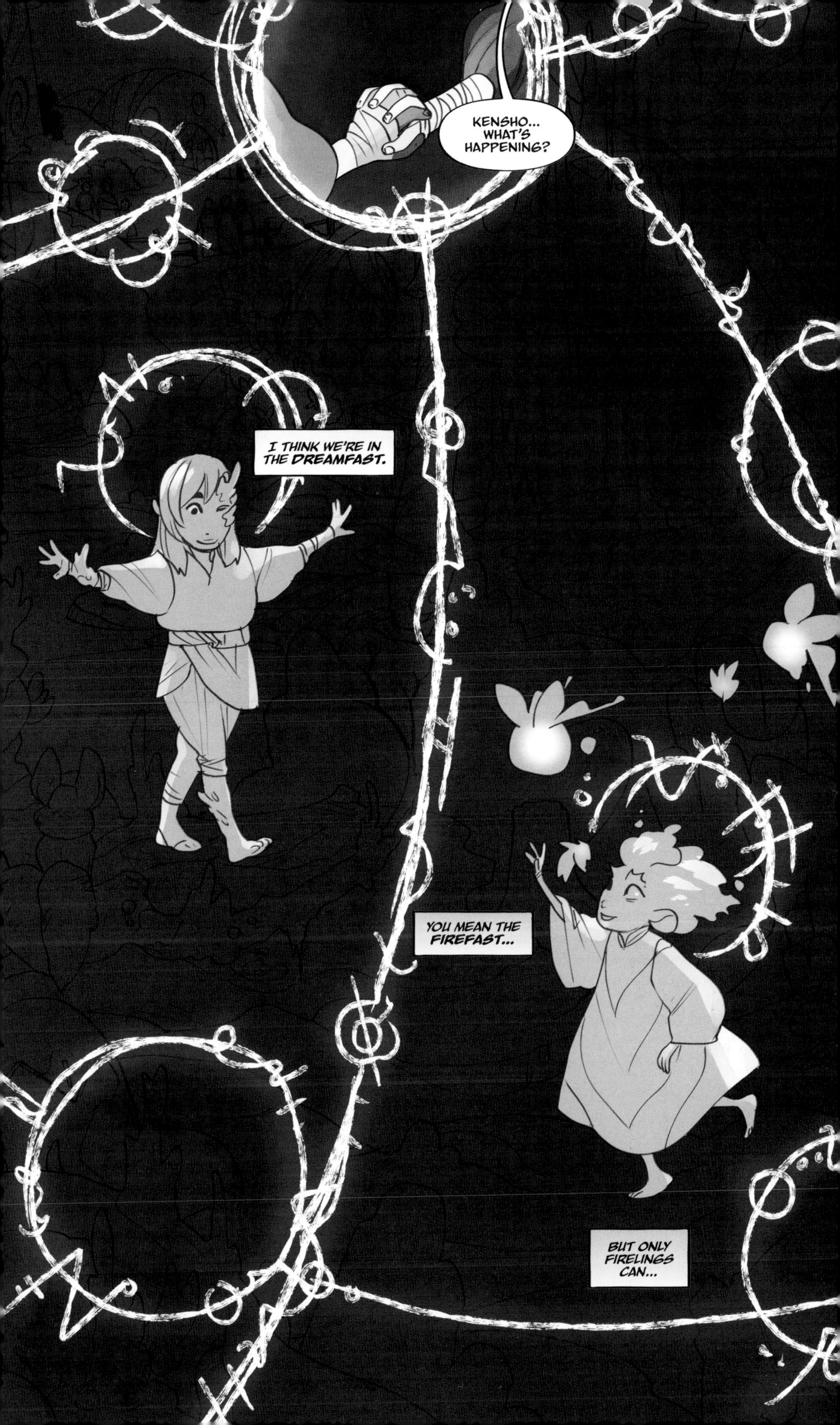
KENSHO... WHAT'S HAPPENING?
I THINK WE'RE IN THE DREAMFAST.
YOU MEAN THE FIREFAST...
BUT ONLY FIRELINGS CAN...

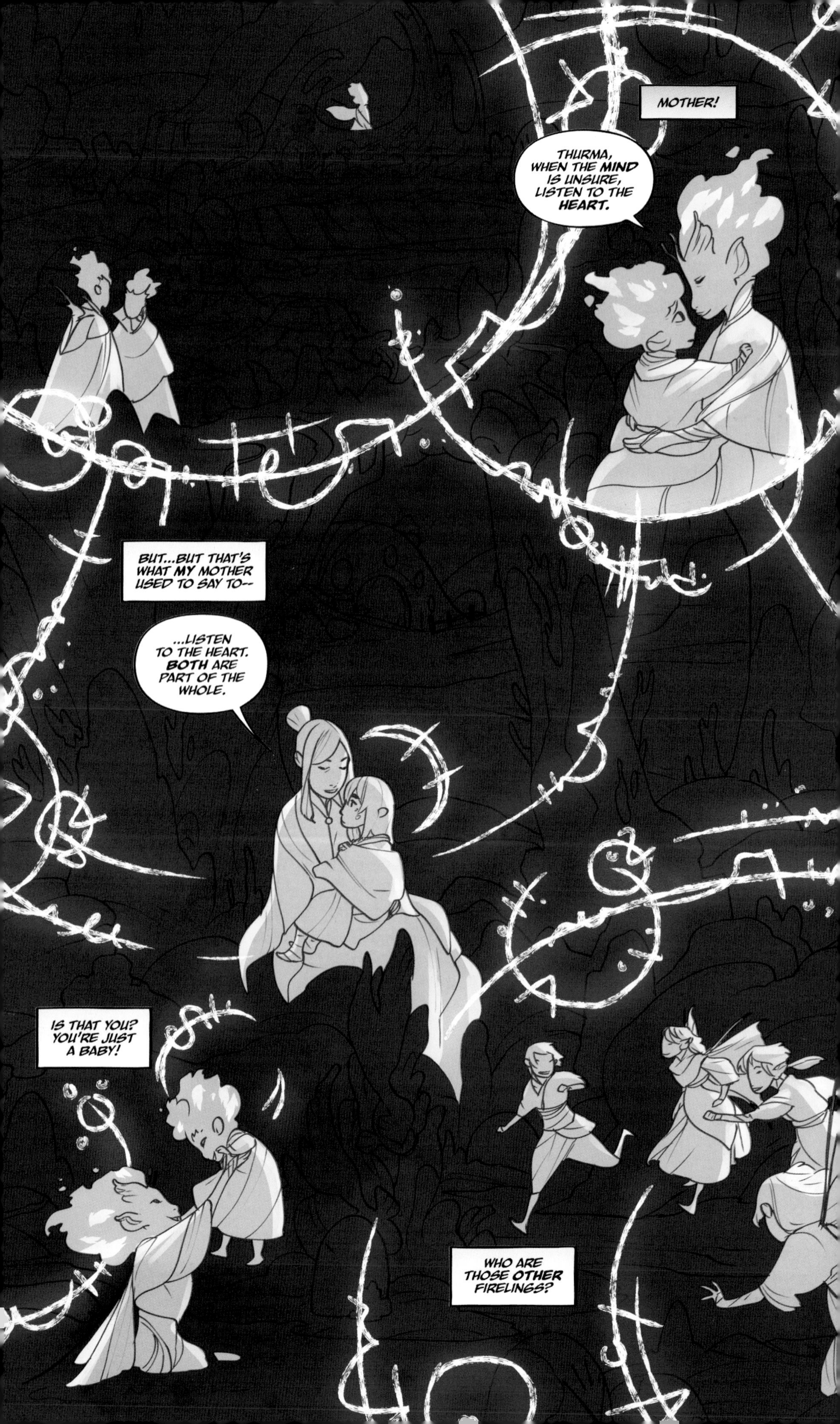
MOTHER!
THURMA, WHEN THE MIND IS UNSURE, LISTEN TO THE HEART.
BUT...BUT THAT'S WHAT MY MOTHER USED TO SAY TO--
...LISTEN TO THE HEART. BOTH ARE PART OF THE WHOLE.
IS THAT YOU? YOU'RE JUST A BABY!
WHO ARE THOSE OTHER FIRELINGS?

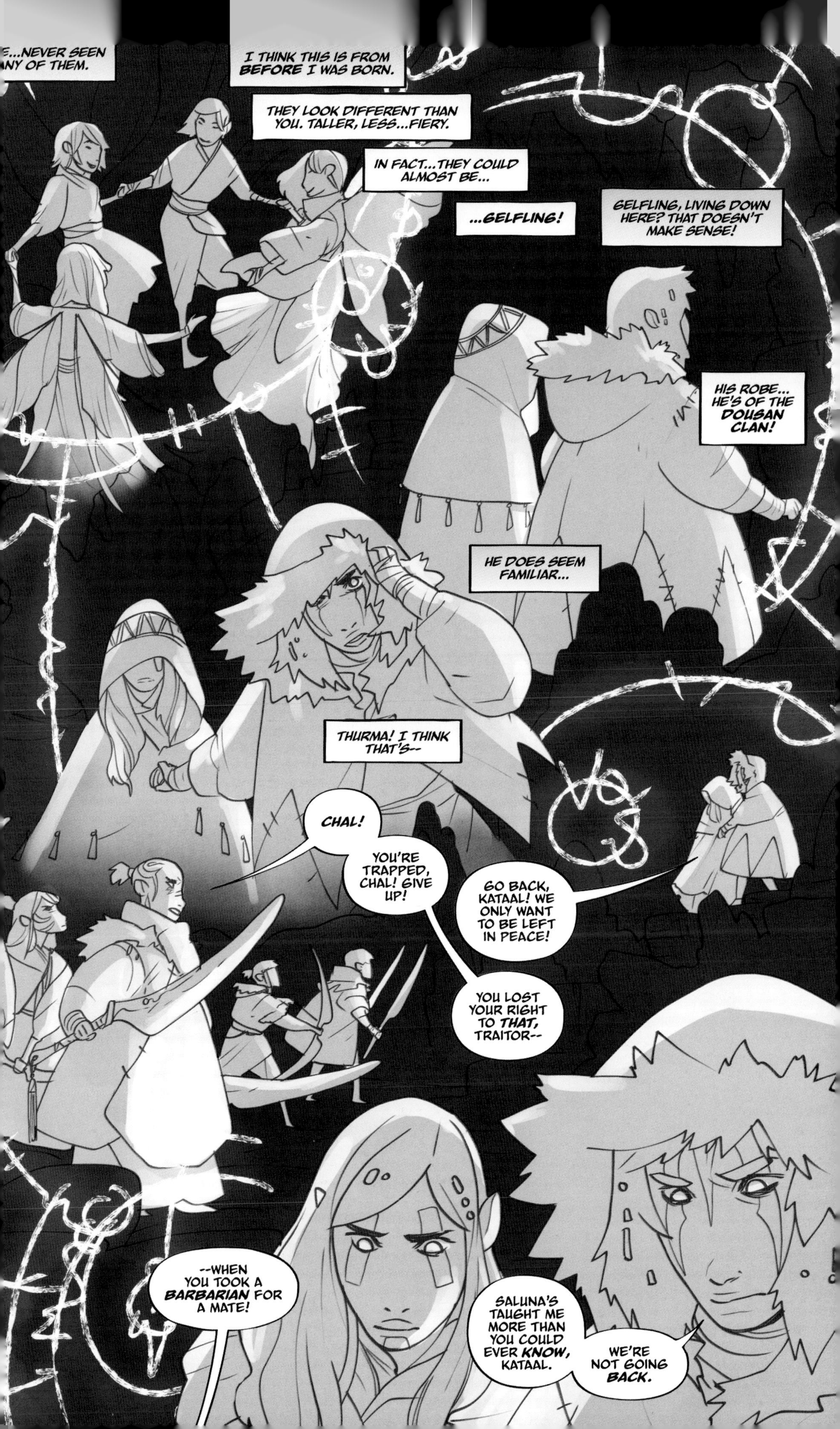

E...NEVER SEEN
ANY OF THEM.
I THINK THIS IS FROM BEFORE I WAS BORN.
THEY LOOK DIFFERENT THAN YOU. TALLER, LESS...FIERY.
IN FACT...THEY COULD ALMOST BE...
...GELFLING!
GELFLING, LIVING DOWN HERE? THAT DOESN'T MAKE SENSE!
HIS ROBE... HE'S OF THE DOUSAN CLAN!
HE DOES SEEM FAMILIAR...
THURMA! I THINK THAT'S--
CHAL!
YOU'RE TRAPPED, CHAL! GIVE UP!
GO BACK, KATAAL! WE ONLY WANT TO BE LEFT IN PEACE!
YOU LOST YOUR RIGHT TO THAT, TRAITOR--
--WHEN YOU TOOK A BARBARIAN FOR A MATE!
SALUNA'S TAUGHT ME MORE THAN YOU COULD EVER KNOW, KATAAL.
WE'RE NOT GOING BACK.

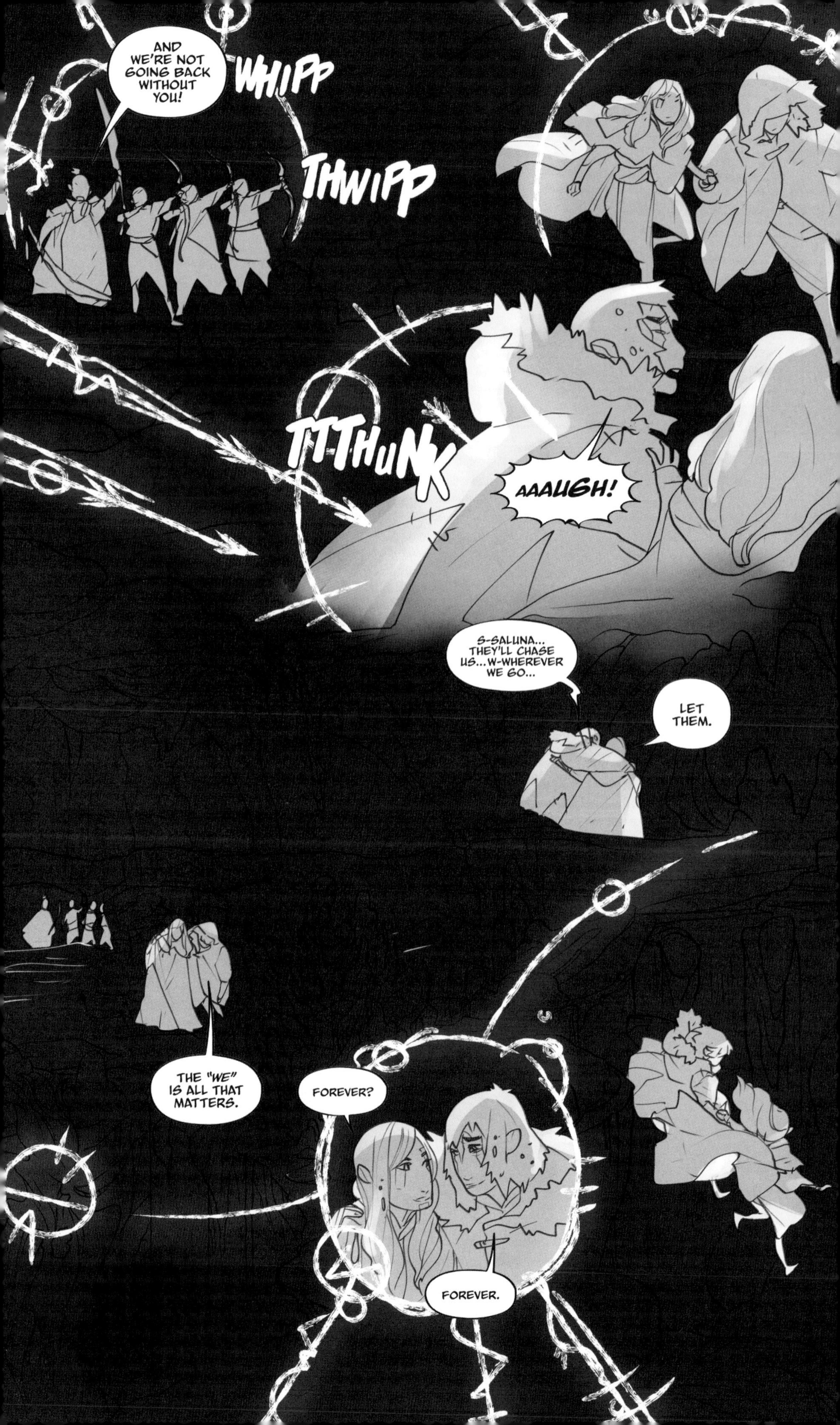

AND WE'RE NOT GOING BACK WITHOUT YOU!
WHIPP
THWIPP
TTTHUNK
AAAUGH!
S-SALUNA... THEY'LL CHASE US...W-WHEREVER WE GO...
LET THEM.
THE "WE" IS ALL THAT MATTERS.
FOREVER?
FOREVER.

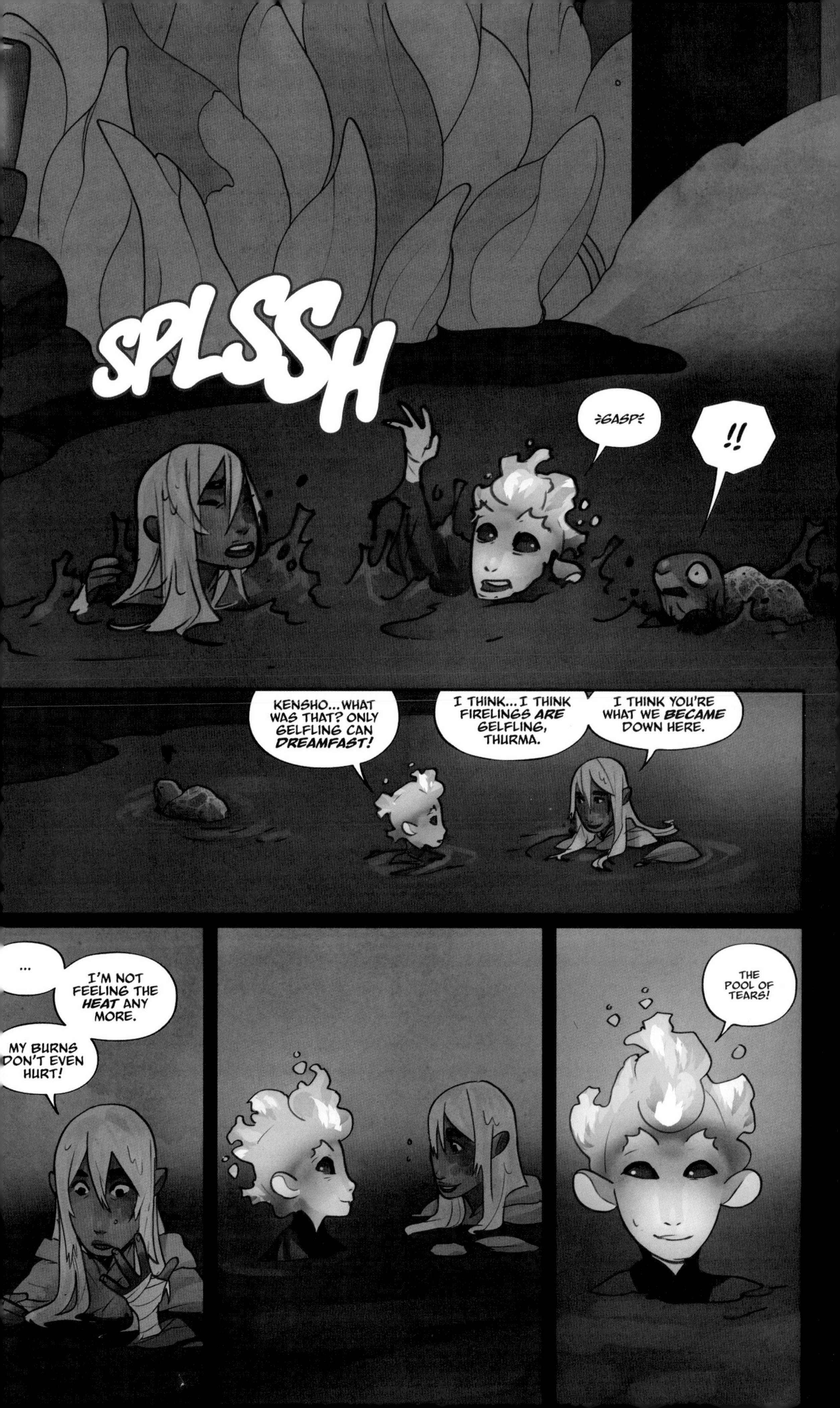
SPLSSH
GASP
!!
KENSHO...WHAT WAS THAT? ONLY GELFLING CAN DREAMFAST!
I THINK...I THINK FIRELINGS ARE GELFLING, THURMA.
I THINK YOU'RE WHAT WE BECAME DOWN HERE.
...
I'M NOT FEELING THE HEAT ANY MORE.
MY BURNS DON'T EVEN HURT!
THE POOL OF TEARS!

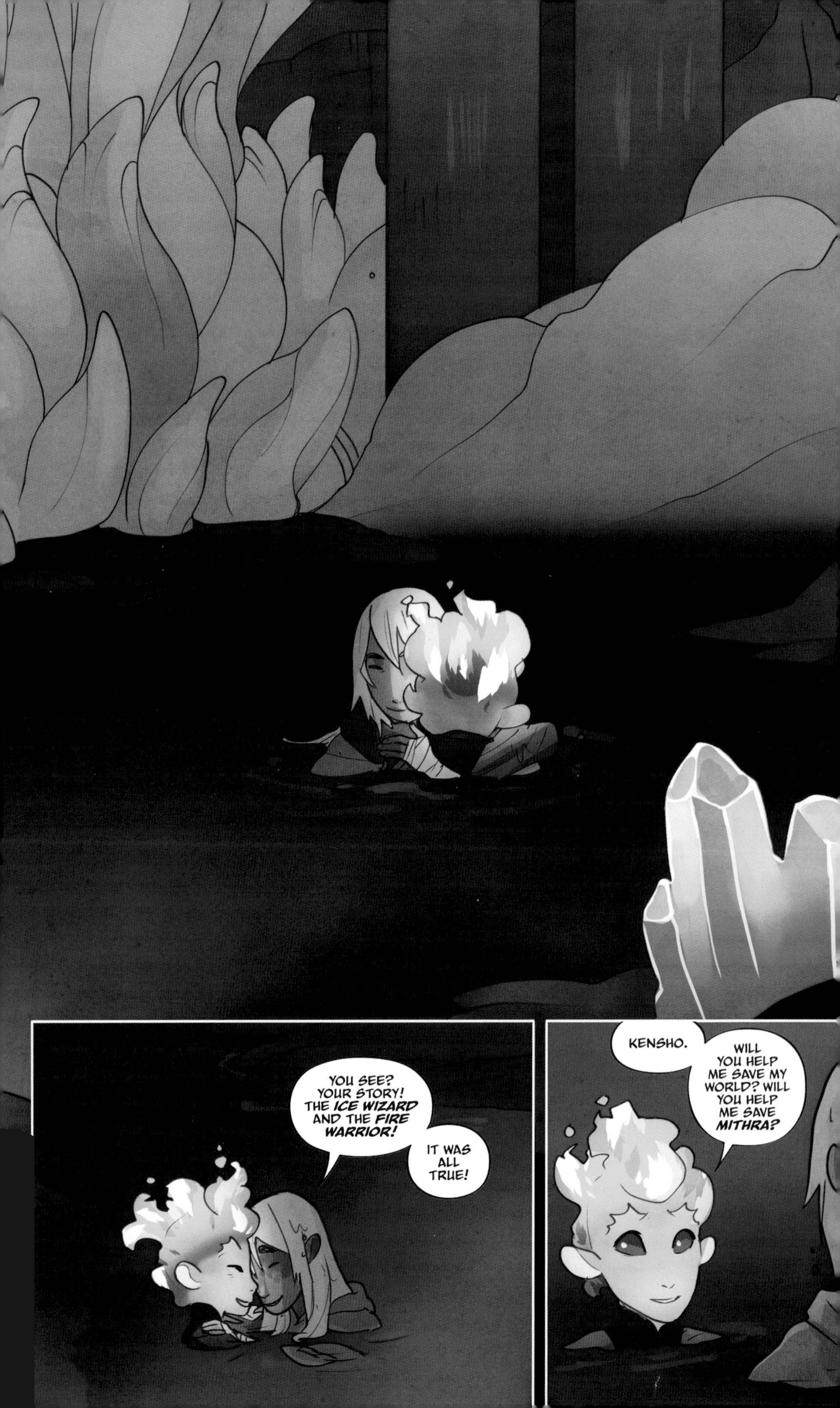
YOU SEE? YOUR STORY! THE ICE WIZARD AND THE FIRE WARRIOR!
IT WAS ALL TRUE!
KENSHO.
WILL YOU HELP ME SAVE MY WORLD? WILL YOU HELP ME SAVE MITHRA?

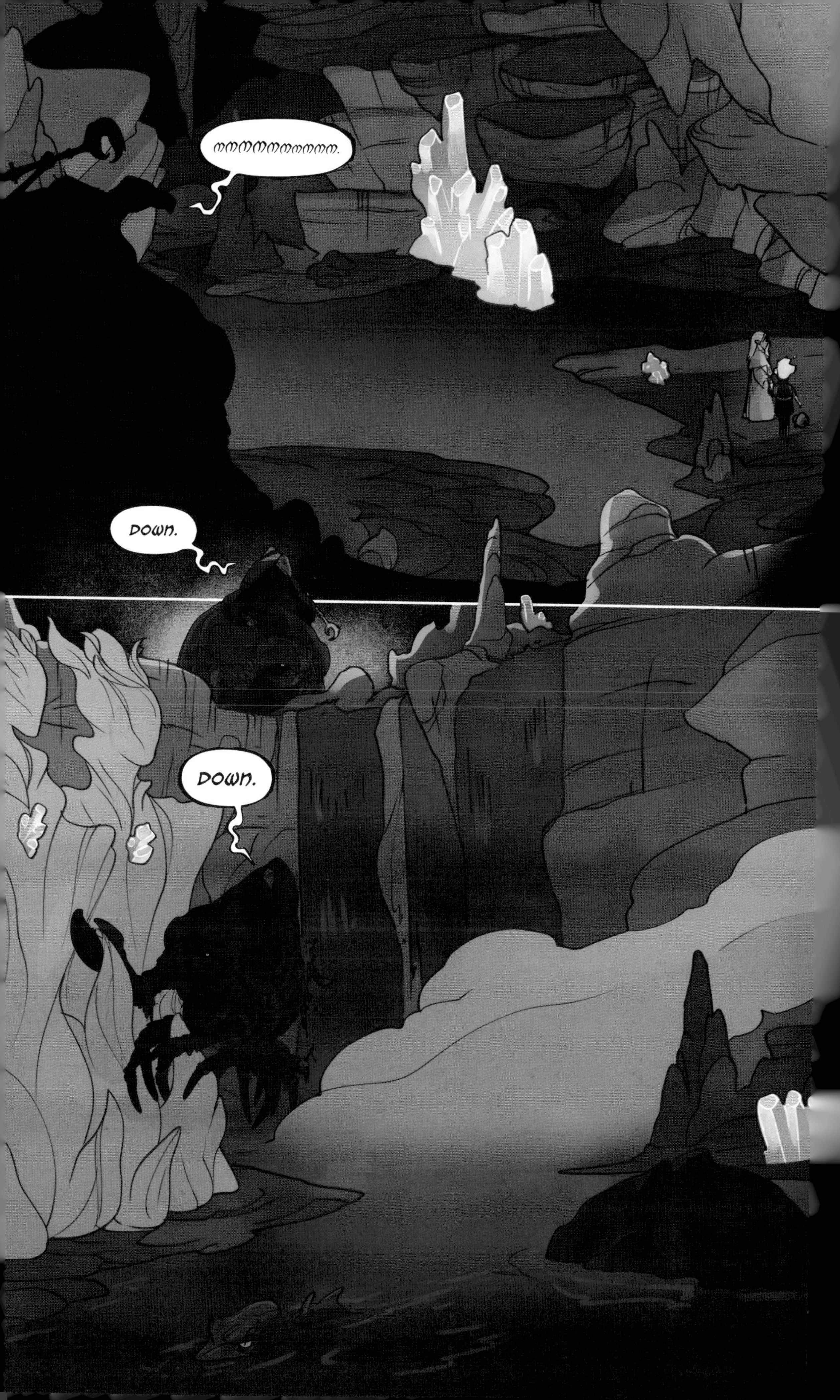
MMMMMMMMMM.
DOWN.
DOWN.

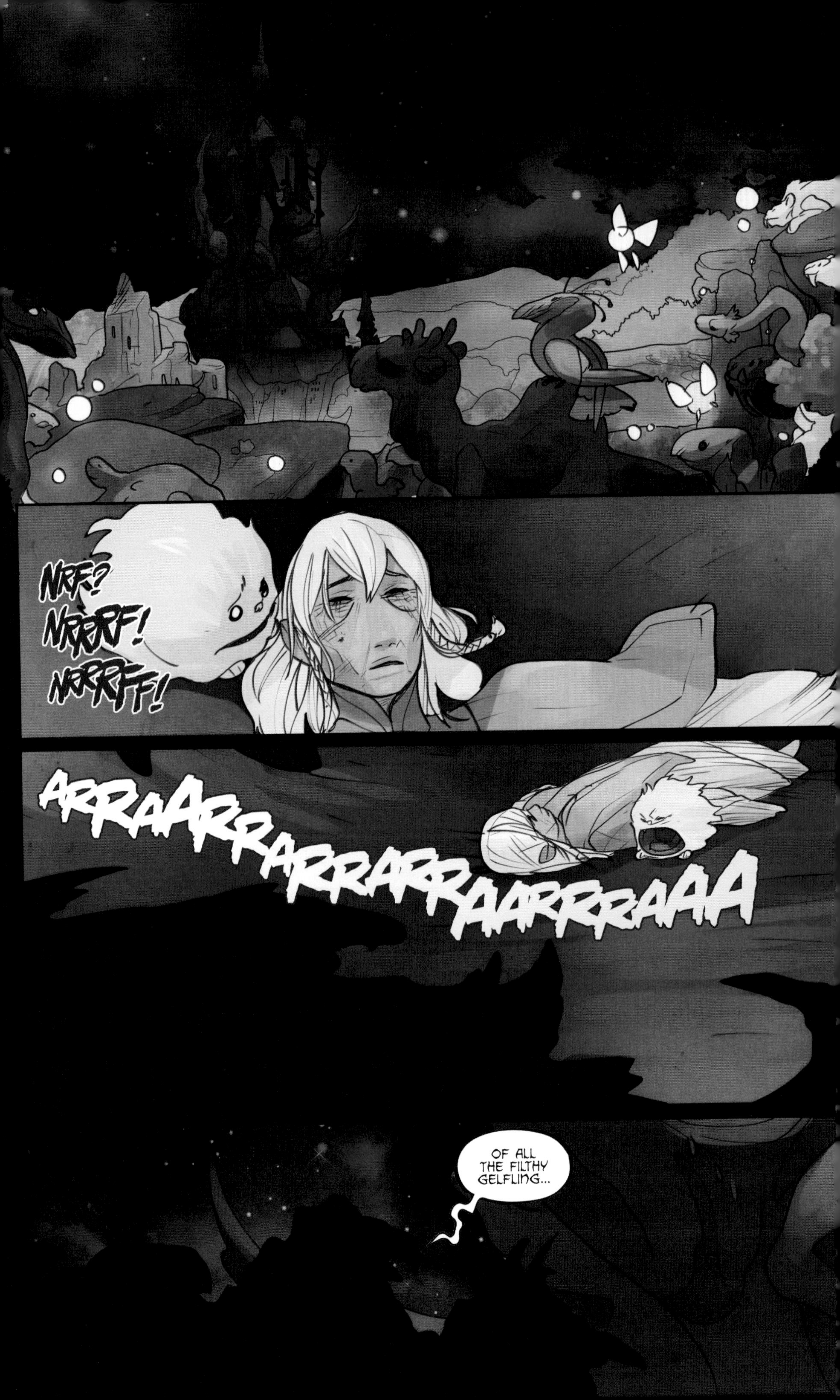

NRF? NRRRF! NRRRFF!
ARRAARRARRARRAARRRAAA
OF ALL THE FILTHY GELFLING...

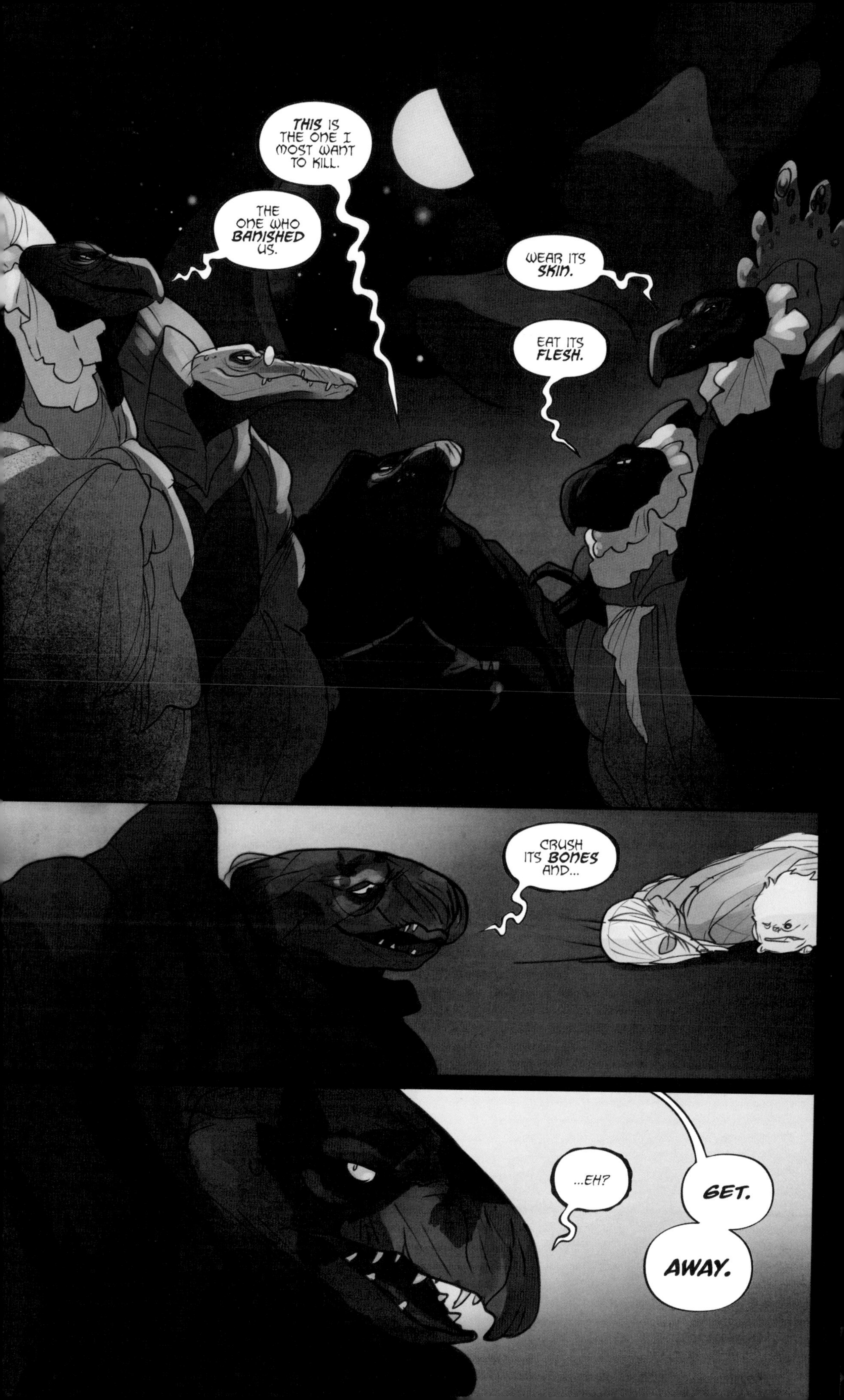
THIS IS THE ONE I MOST WANT TO KILL.
THE ONE WHO BANISHED US.
WEAR ITS SKIN.
EAT ITS FLESH.
CRUSH ITS BONES AND...
...EH?
GET.
AWAY.

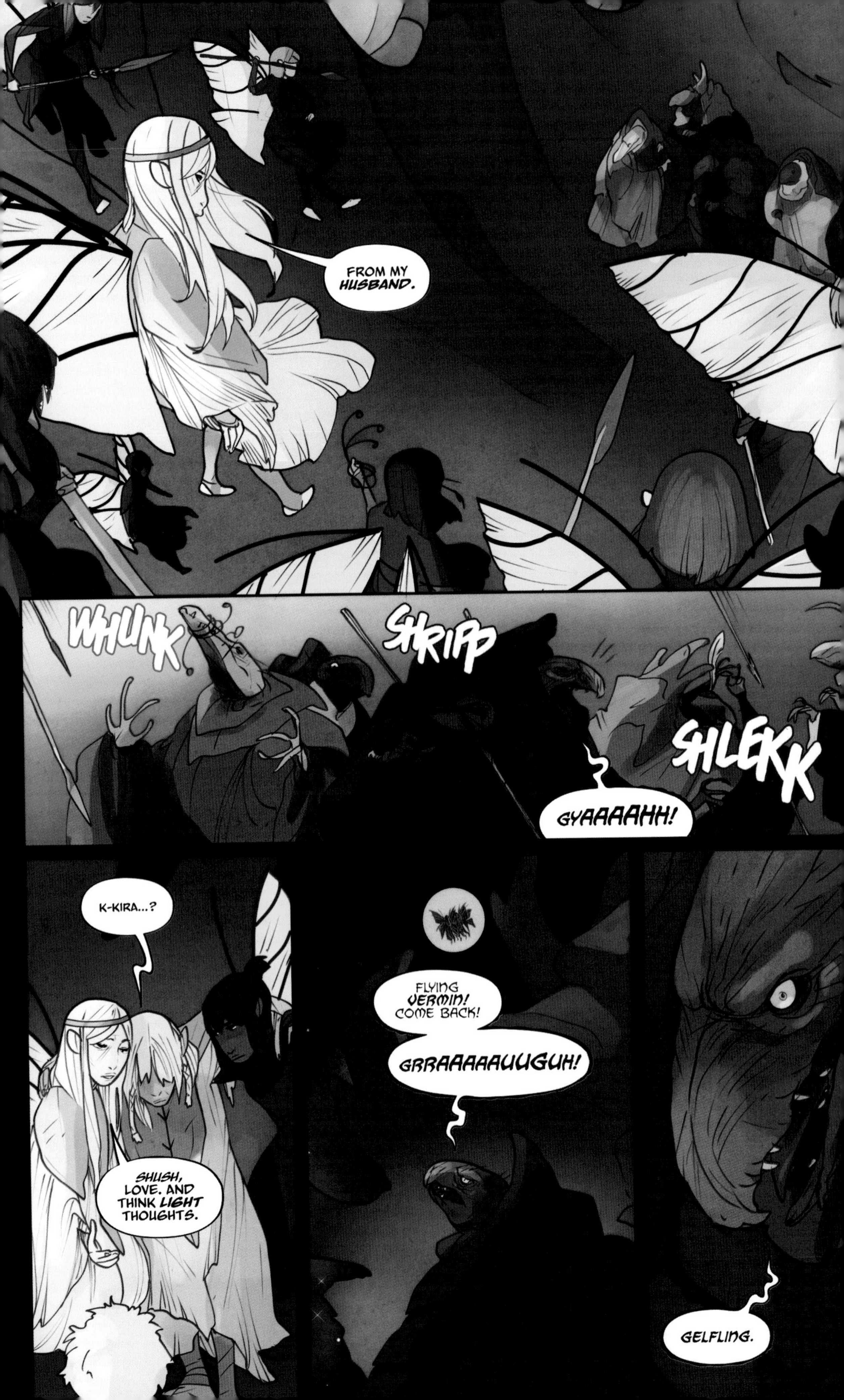
FROM MY HUSBAND.
WHUNK
SHRIPP
SHLEKK
GYAAAAHH!
K-KIRA...?
SHUSH, LOVE. AND THINK LIGHT THOUGHTS.
FLYING VERMIN! COME BACK!
GRRAAAAAUUGUH!
GELFLING.

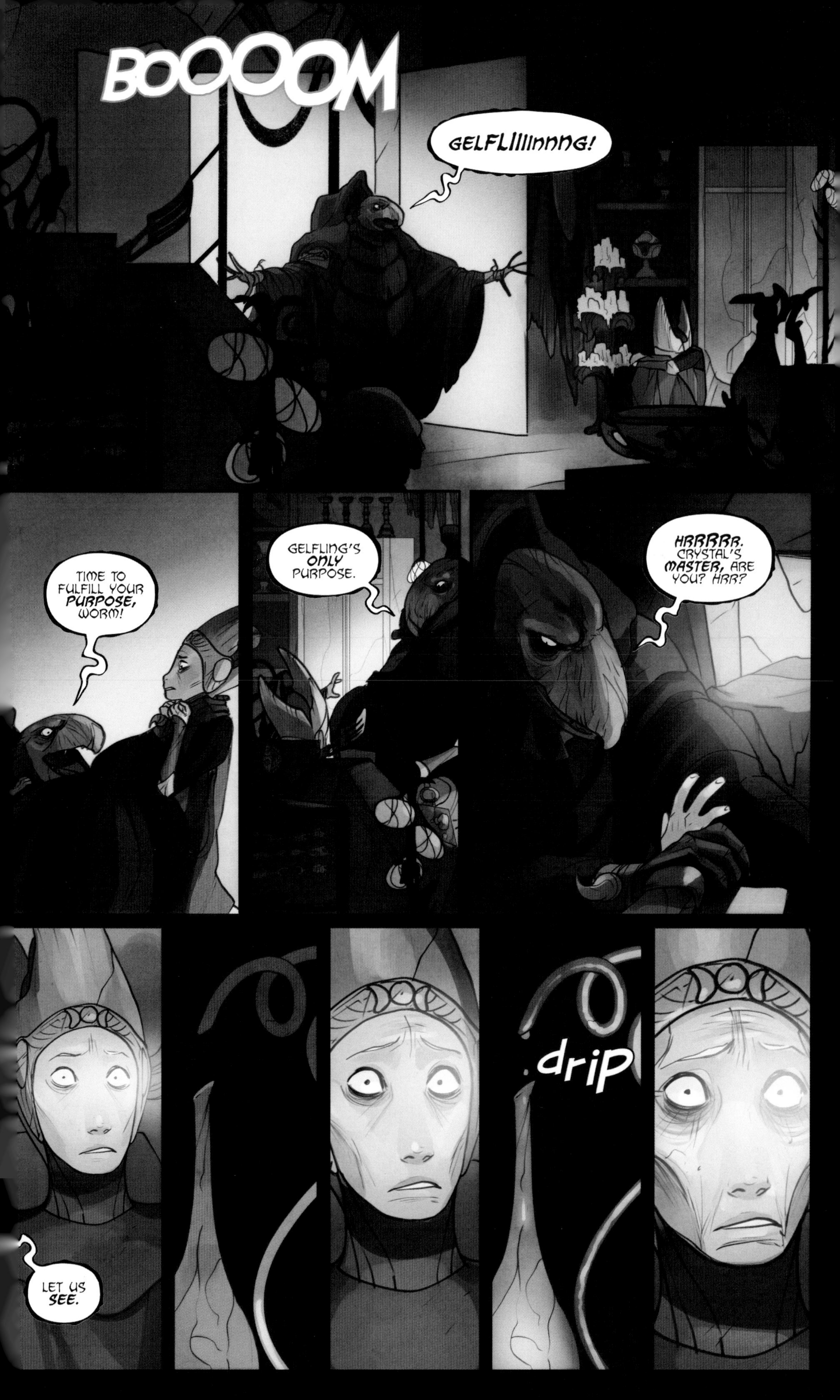
BOOOOM
GELFLIIIIinnnG!
TIME TO FULFILL YOUR PURPOSE, WORM!
GELFLING'S ONLY PURPOSE.
HRRRRR. CRYSTAL'S MASTER, ARE YOU? HRR?
LET US SEE.
drip

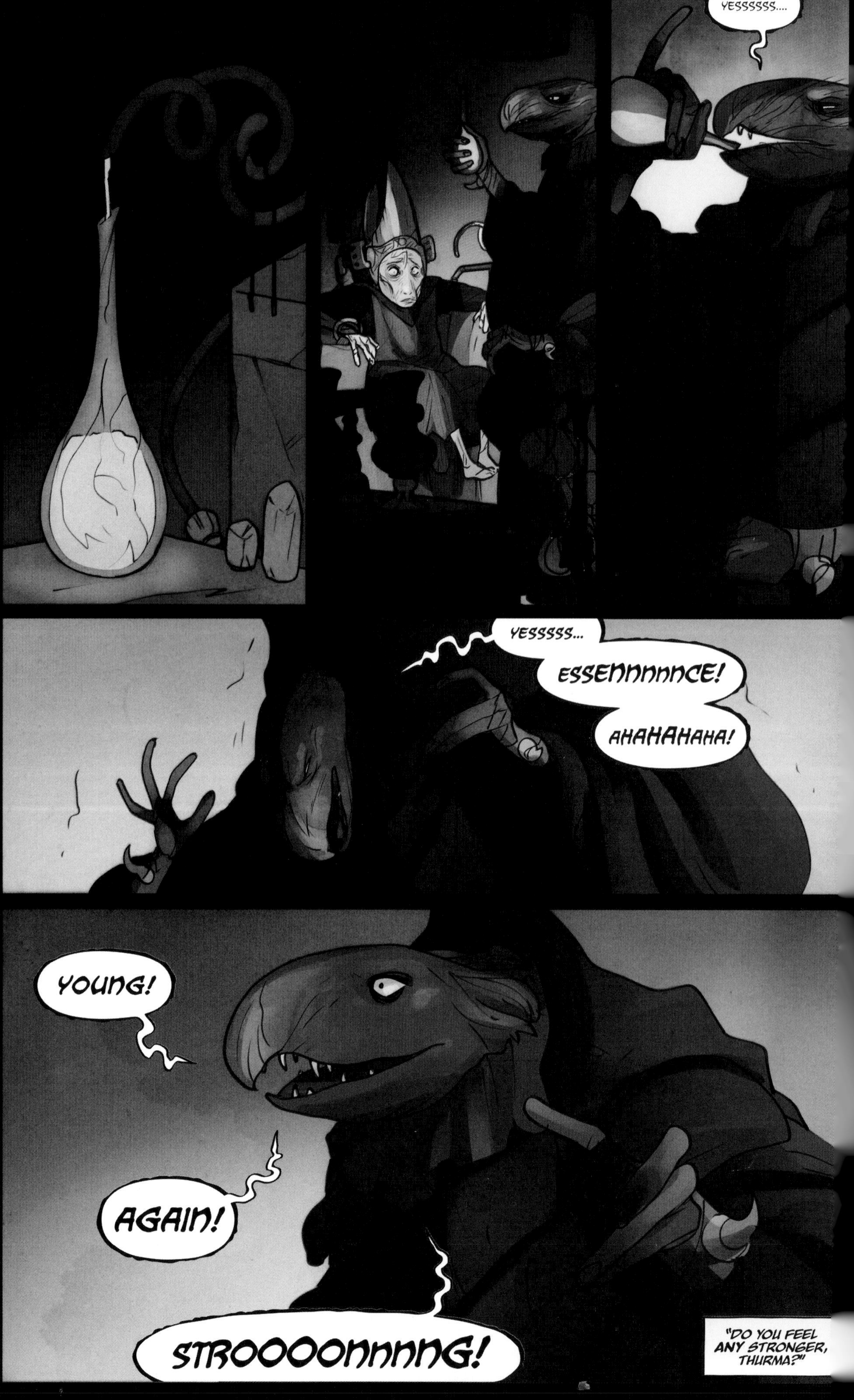
YESSSSSS....
YESSSSS...
ESSENNNNNCE!
AHAHAHAHA!
YOUNG!
AGAIN!
STROOOONNNNG!
"DO YOU FEEL ANY STRONGER, THURMA?"

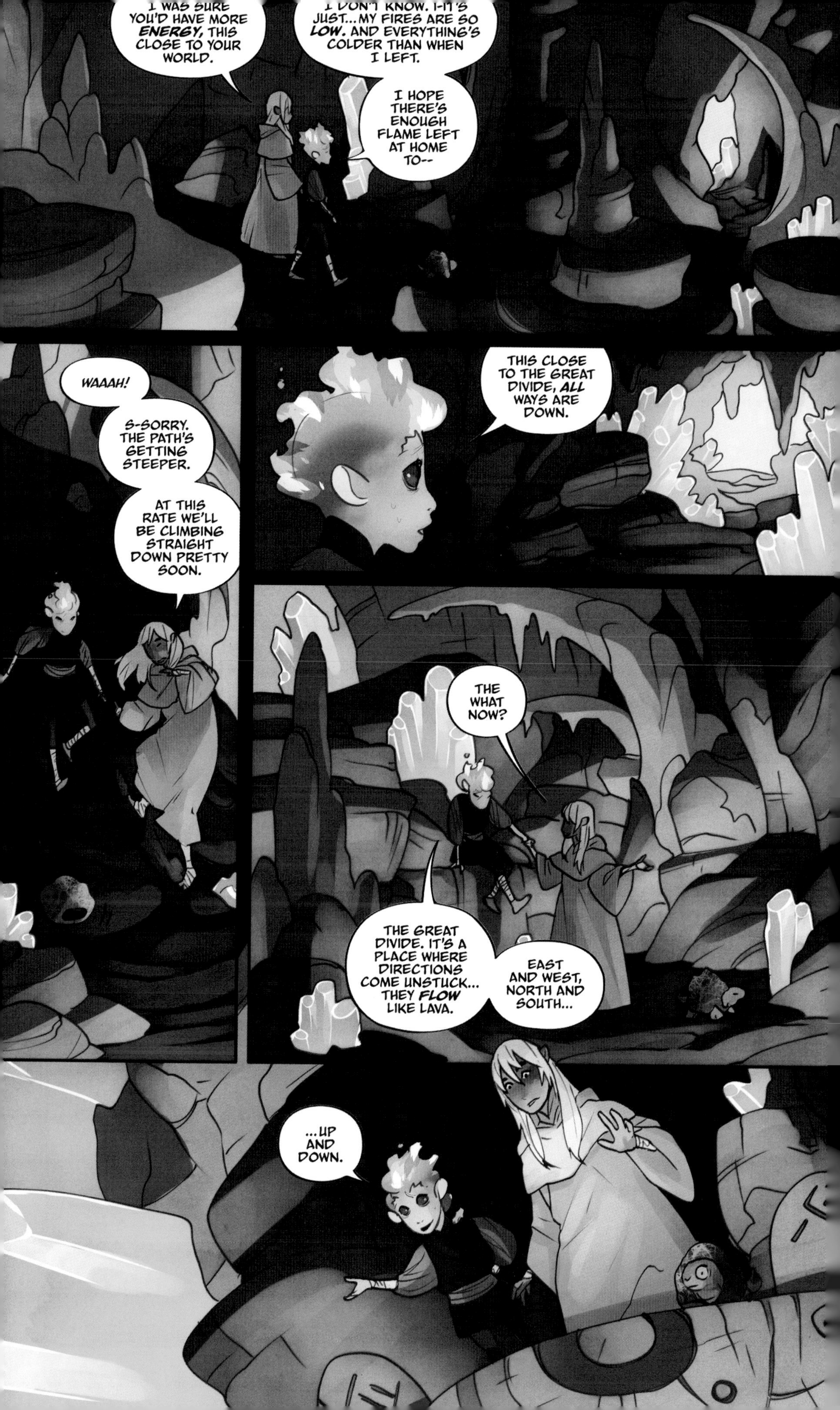
I WAS SURE YOU'D HAVE MORE ENERGY, THIS CLOSE TO YOUR WORLD.
I DON'T KNOW. I-IT'S JUST... MY FIRES ARE SO LOW. AND EVERYTHING'S COLDER THAN WHEN I LEFT.
I HOPE THERE'S ENOUGH FLAME LEFT AT HOME TO--
WAAAH!
S-SORRY. THE PATH'S GETTING STEEPER.
AT THIS RATE WE'LL BE CLIMBING STRAIGHT DOWN PRETTY SOON.
THIS CLOSE TO THE GREAT DIVIDE, ALL WAYS ARE DOWN.
THE WHAT NOW?
THE GREAT DIVIDE. IT'S A PLACE WHERE DIRECTIONS COME UNSTUCK... THEY FLOW LIKE LAVA.
EAST AND WEST, NORTH AND SOUTH...
...UP AND DOWN.

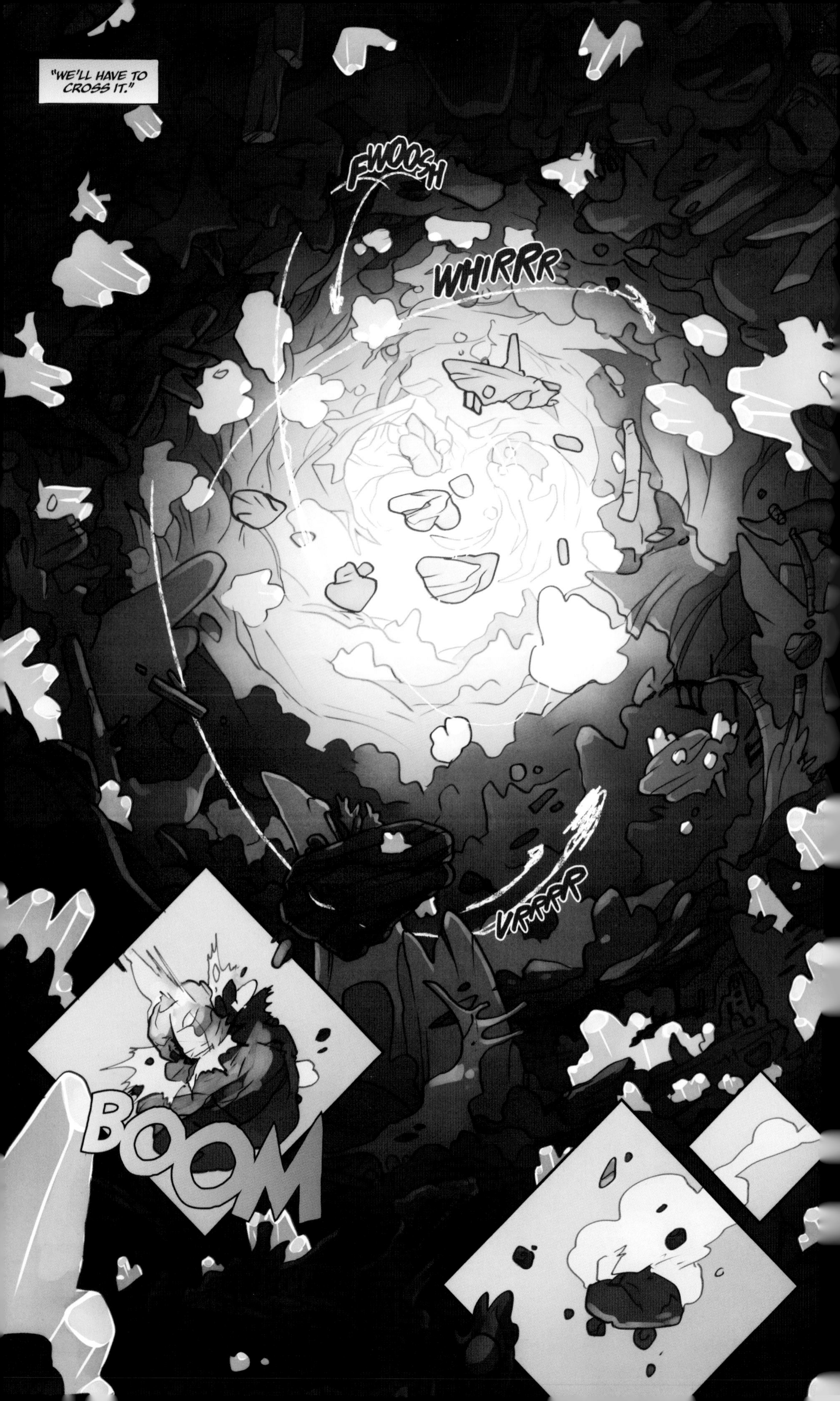
"WE'LL HAVE TO CROSS IT."
FWOOSH
WHIRRR
VRRRR
BOOM

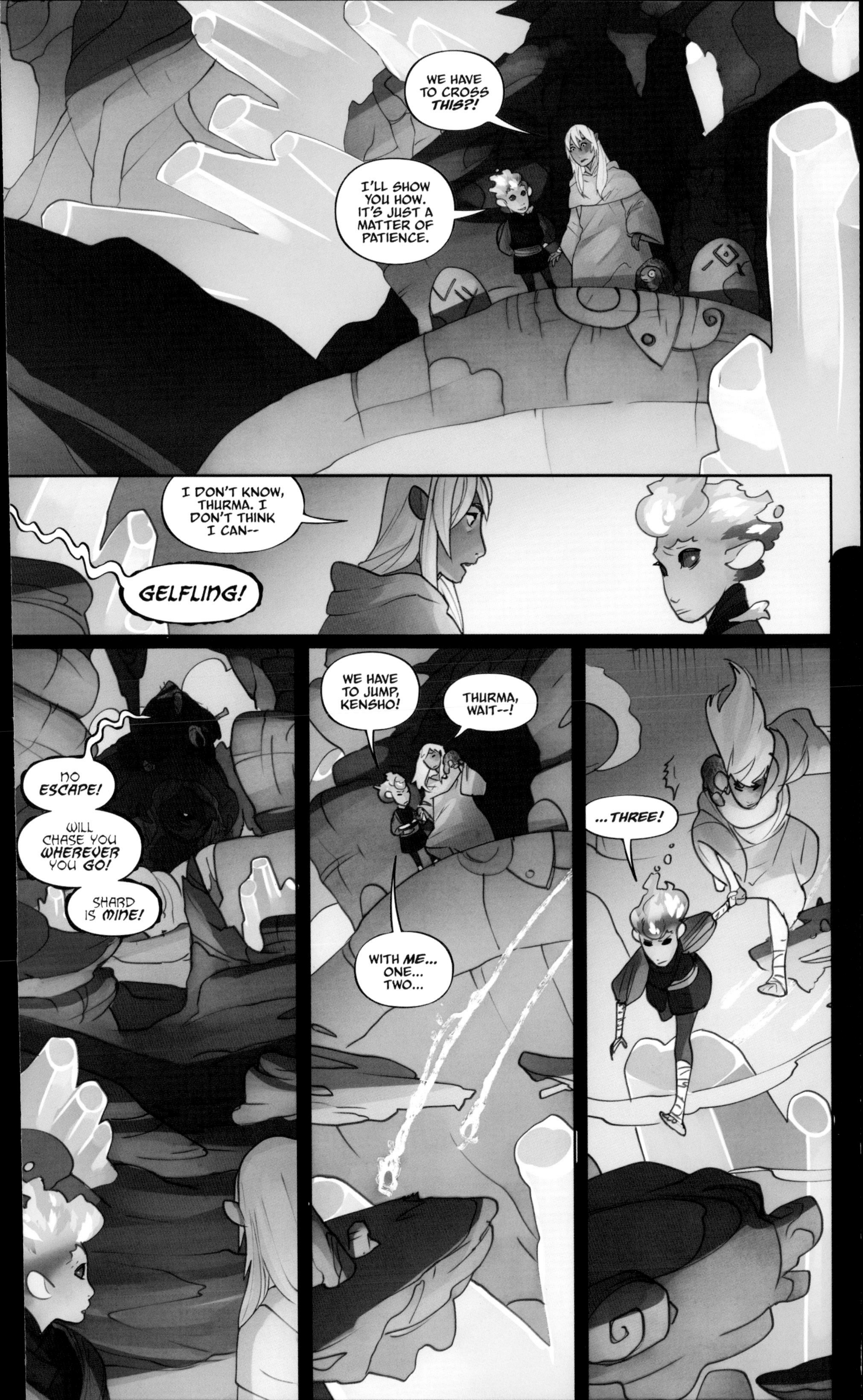
WE HAVE TO CROSS THIS?!
I'LL SHOW YOU HOW. IT'S JUST A MATTER OF PATIENCE.
I DON'T KNOW, THURMA. I DON'T THINK I CAN--
GELFLING!
NO ESCAPE!
WILL CHASE YOU WHEREVER YOU GO!
SHARD IS MINE!
WE HAVE TO JUMP, KENSHO!
THURMA, WAIT--!
WITH ME... ONE... TWO...
...THREE!

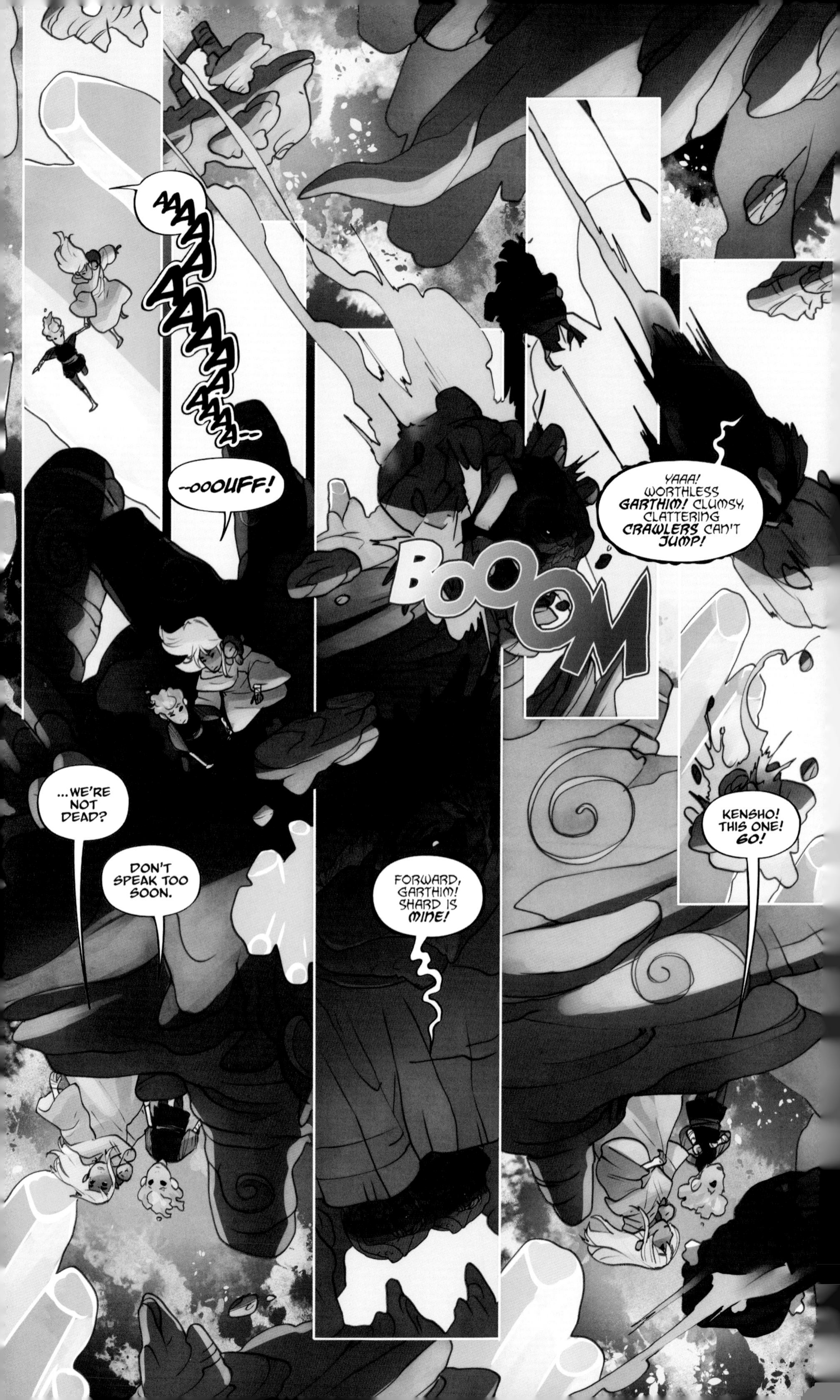
AAAAAAAAAAAAA--
--OOOUFF!
BOOOOM
YAAA! WORTHLESS GARTHIM! CLUMSY, CLATTERING CRAWLERS CAN'T JUMP!
...WE'RE NOT DEAD?
DON'T SPEAK TOO SOON.
FORWARD, GARTHIM! SHARD IS MINE!
KENSHO! THIS ONE! GO!

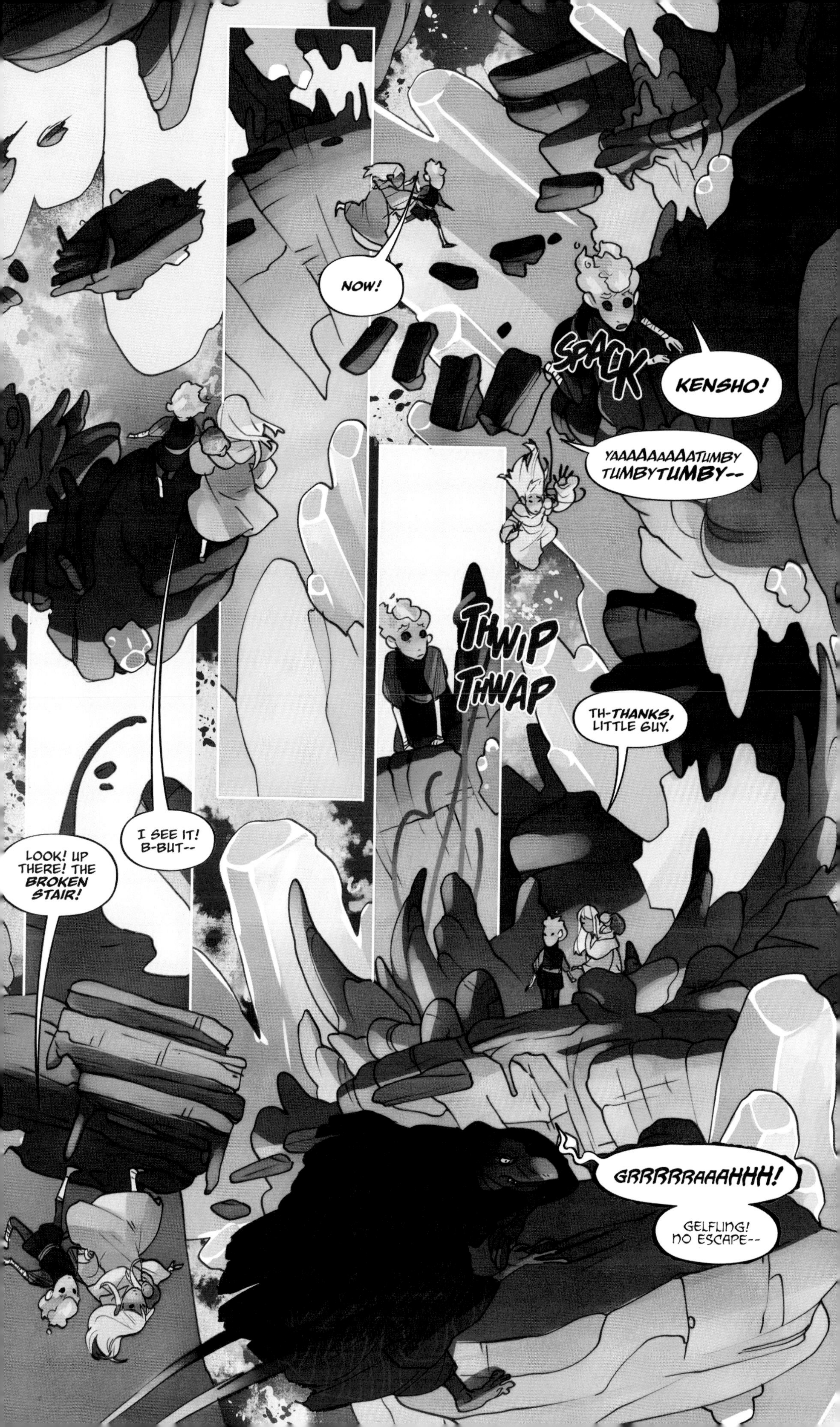
NOW!
SPACK
KENSHO!
YAAAAAAAAATUMBY TUMBYTUMBY--
THWIP
THWAP
TH-THANKS, LITTLE GUY.
LOOK! UP THERE! THE BROKEN STAIR!
I SEE IT! B-BUT--
GRRRRRAAAHHH!
GELFLING! NO ESCAPE--

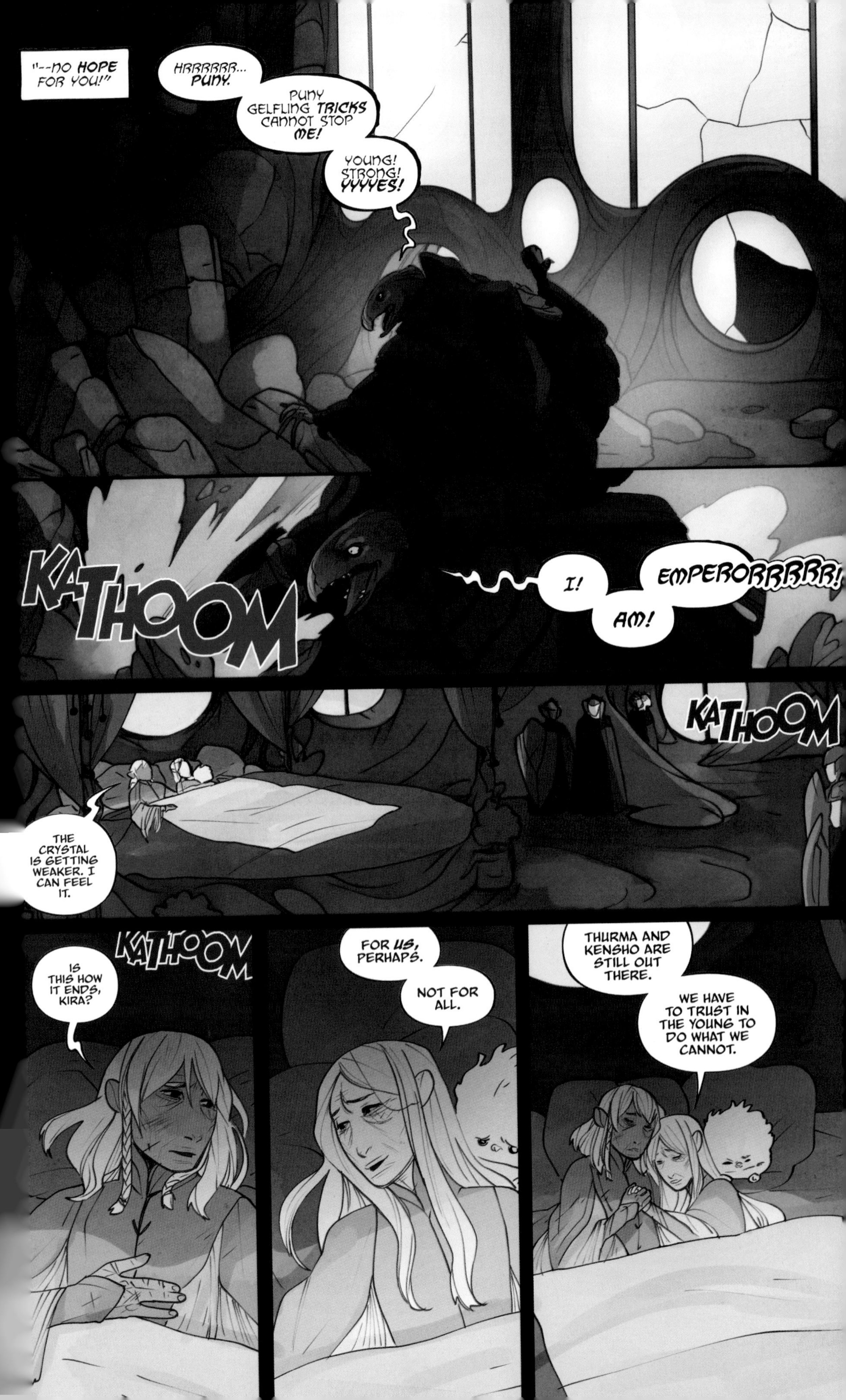
"--NO HOPE FOR YOU!"
HRRRRRR... PUNY.
PUNY GELFLING TRICKS CANNOT STOP ME!
YOUNG! STRONG! YYYYES!
KATHOOM
I!
AM!
EMPERORRRRRR!
KATHOOM
THE CRYSTAL IS GETTING WEAKER. I CAN FEEL IT.
KATHOOM
IS THIS HOW IT ENDS, KIRA?
FOR US, PERHAPS.
NOT FOR ALL.
THURMA AND KENSHO ARE STILL OUT THERE.
WE HAVE TO TRUST IN THE YOUNG TO DO WHAT WE CANNOT.

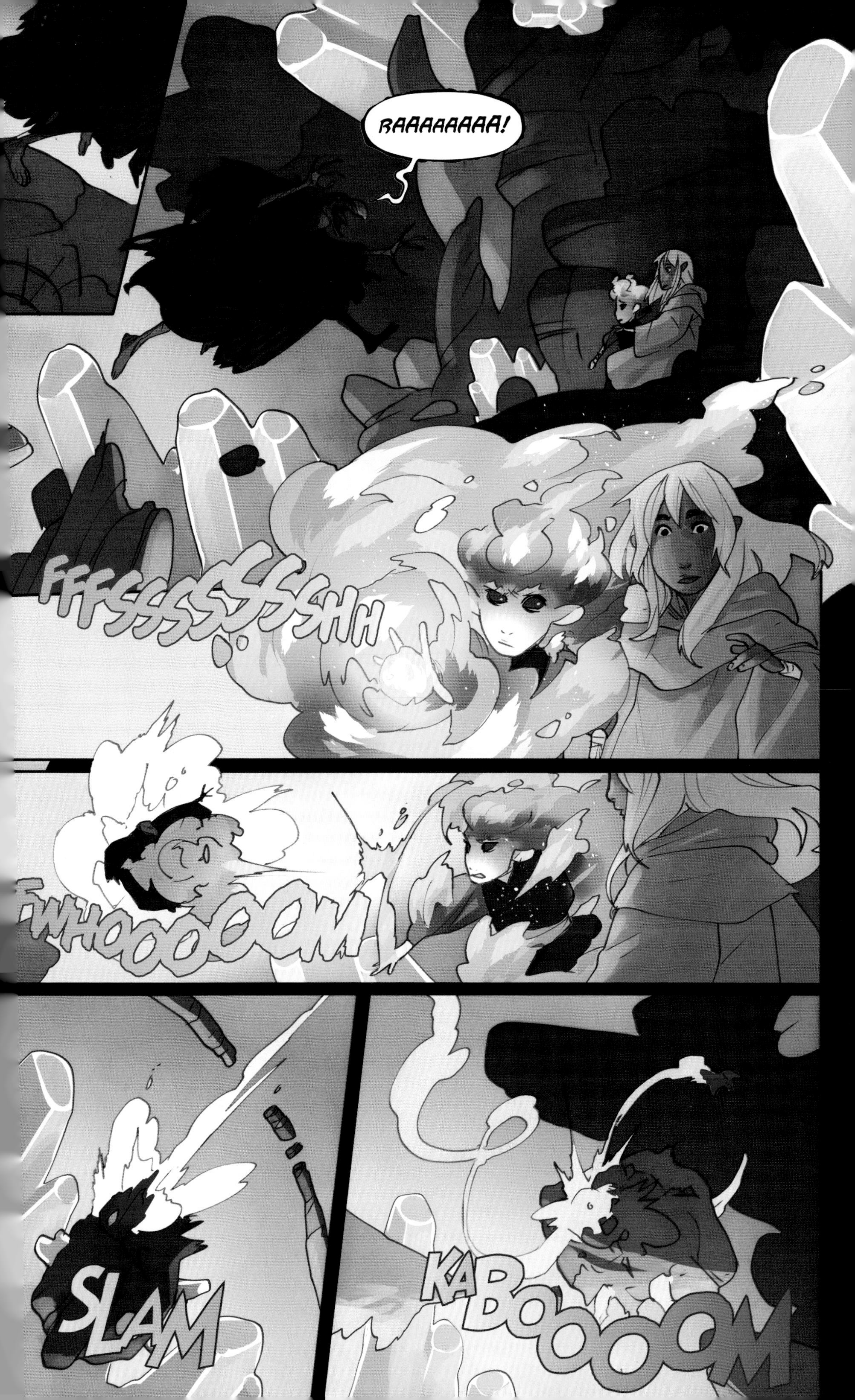
RAAAAAAAA!
FFFSSSSSSSSHH
FWHOOOOOM
SLAM
KABOOOOOM

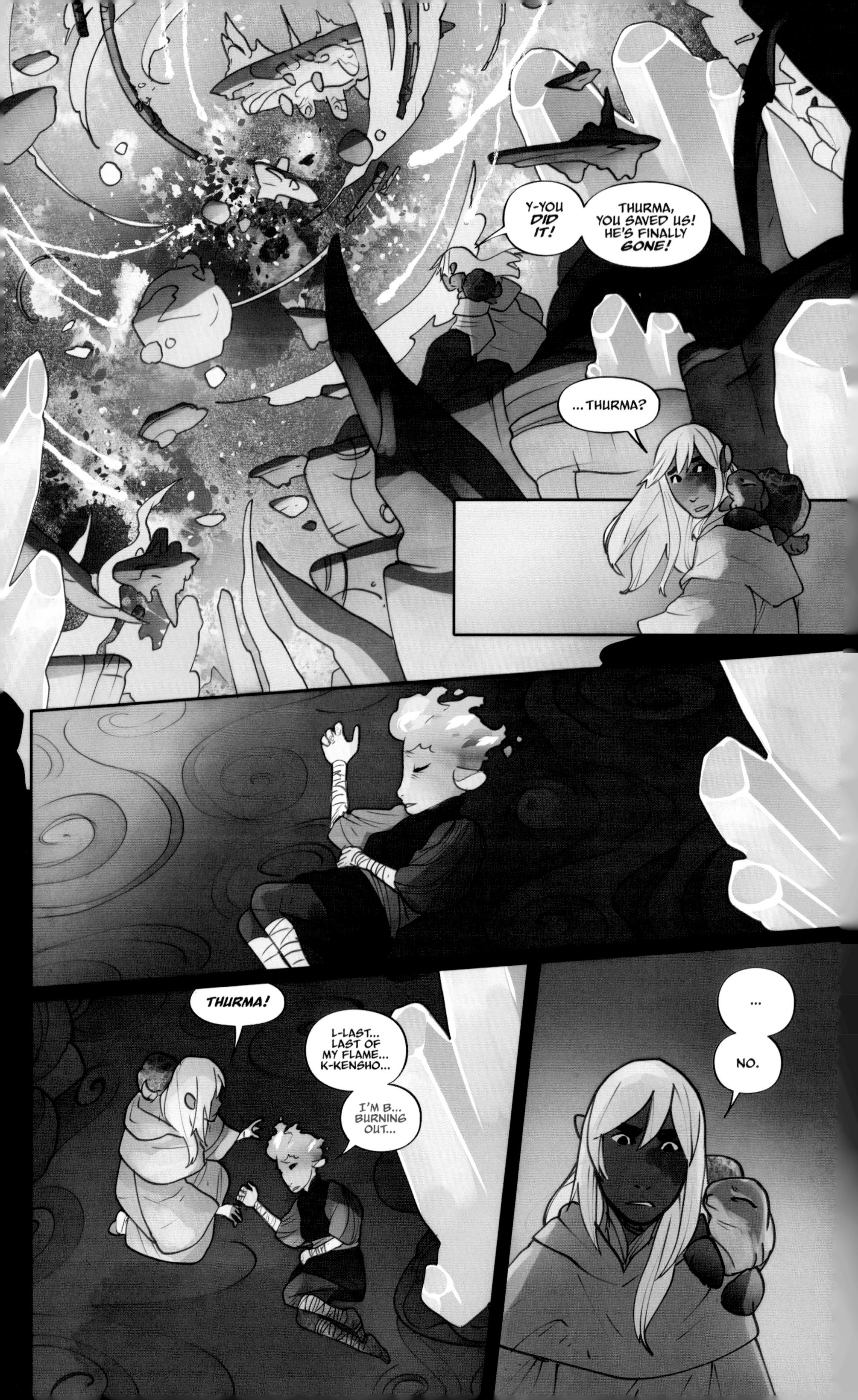
Y-YOU DID IT!
THURMA, YOU SAVED US! HE'S FINALLY GONE!
...THURMA?
THURMA!
L-LAST... LAST OF MY FLAME... K-KENSHO...
I'M B... BURNING OUT...
...
NO.

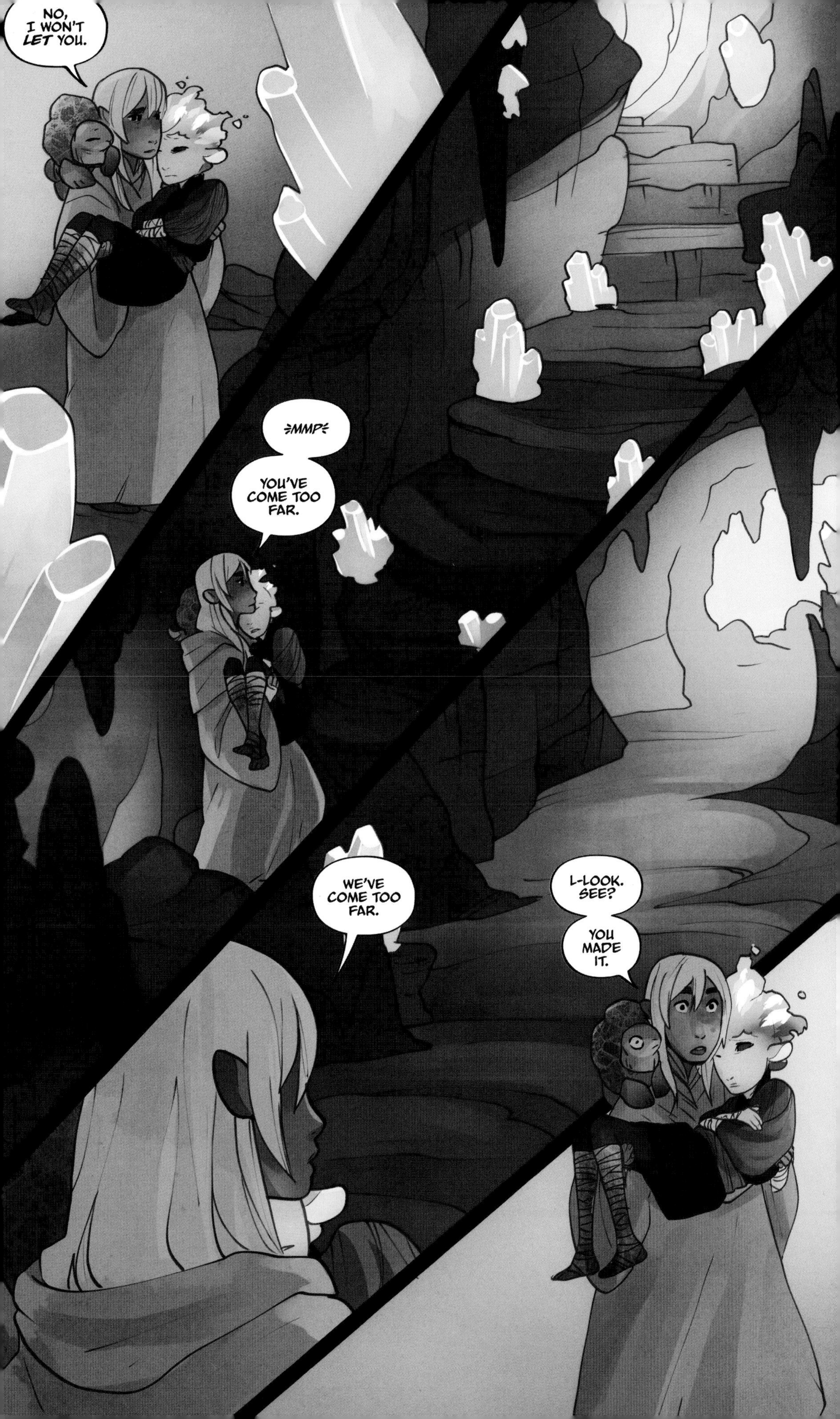
NO, I WON'T *LET* YOU.
⇛MMP⇚
YOU'VE COME TOO FAR.
WE'VE COME TOO FAR.
L-LOOK. SEE?
YOU MADE IT.

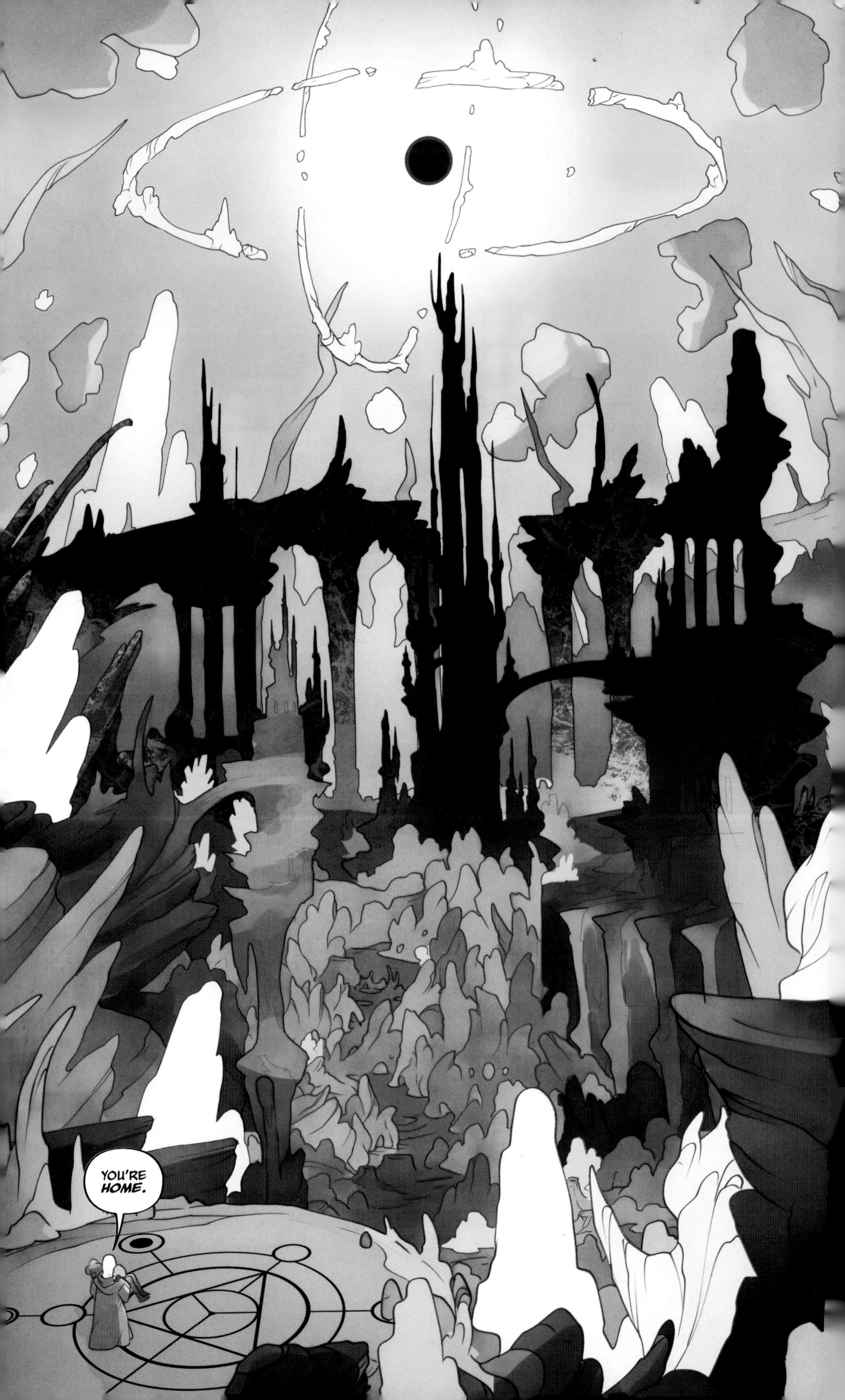
YOU'RE HOME.

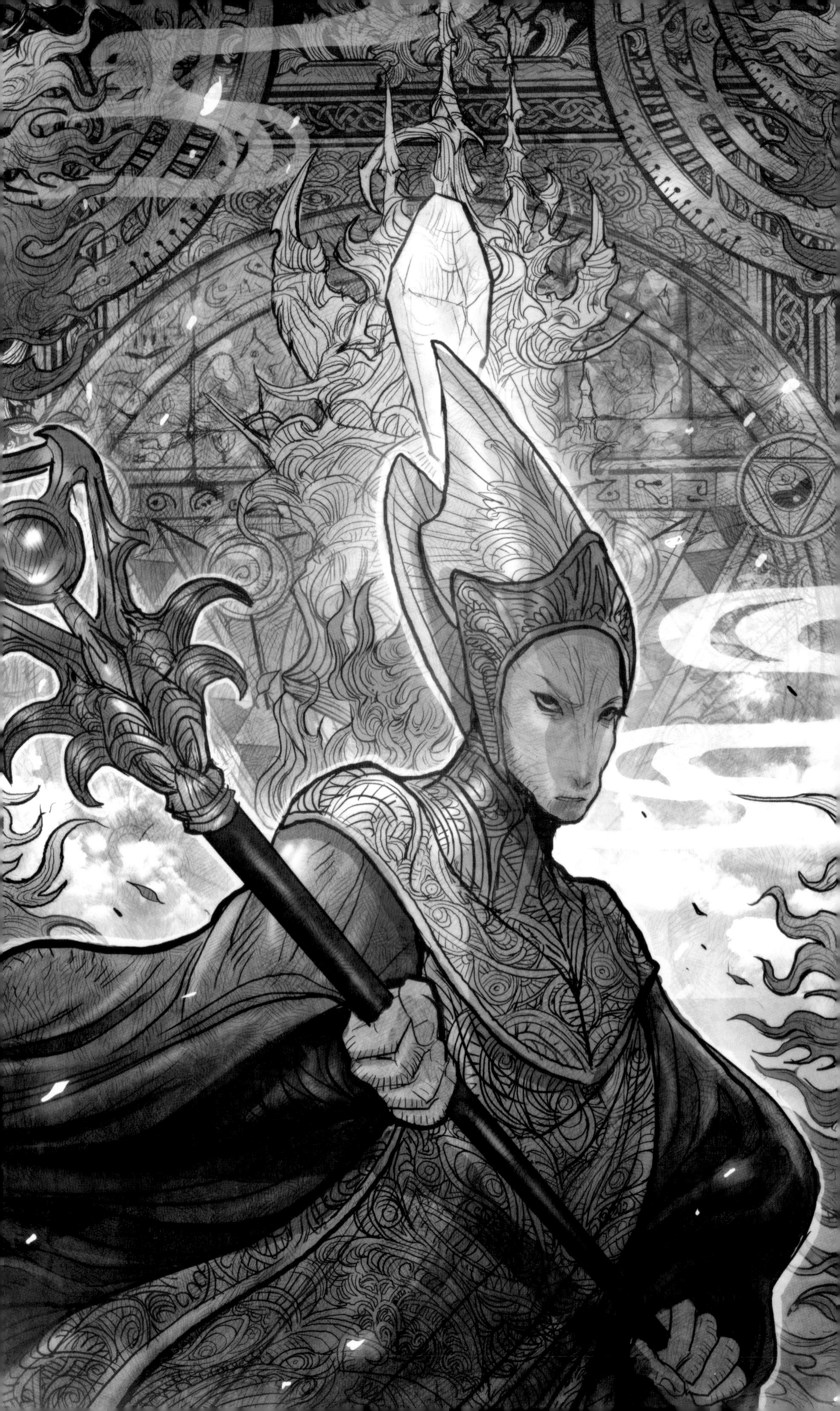

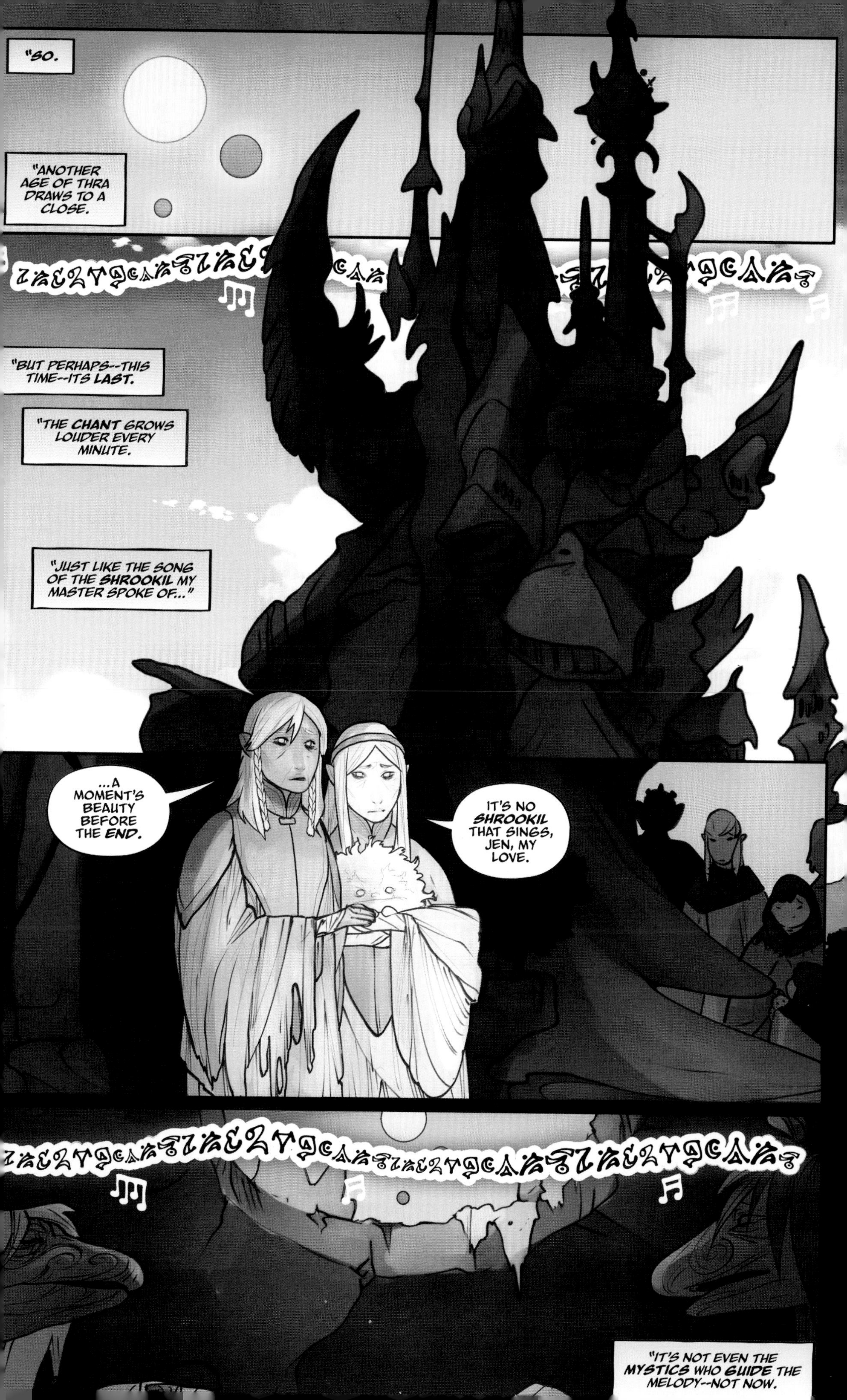
"SO.
"ANOTHER AGE OF THRA DRAWS TO A CLOSE.
"BUT PERHAPS--THIS TIME--ITS LAST.
"THE CHANT GROWS LOUDER EVERY MINUTE.
"JUST LIKE THE SONG OF THE SHROOKIL MY MASTER SPOKE OF..."
...A MOMENT'S BEAUTY BEFORE THE END.
IT'S NO SHROOKIL THAT SINGS, JEN, MY LOVE.
"IT'S NOT EVEN THE MYSTICS WHO GUIDE THE MELODY--NOT NOW.

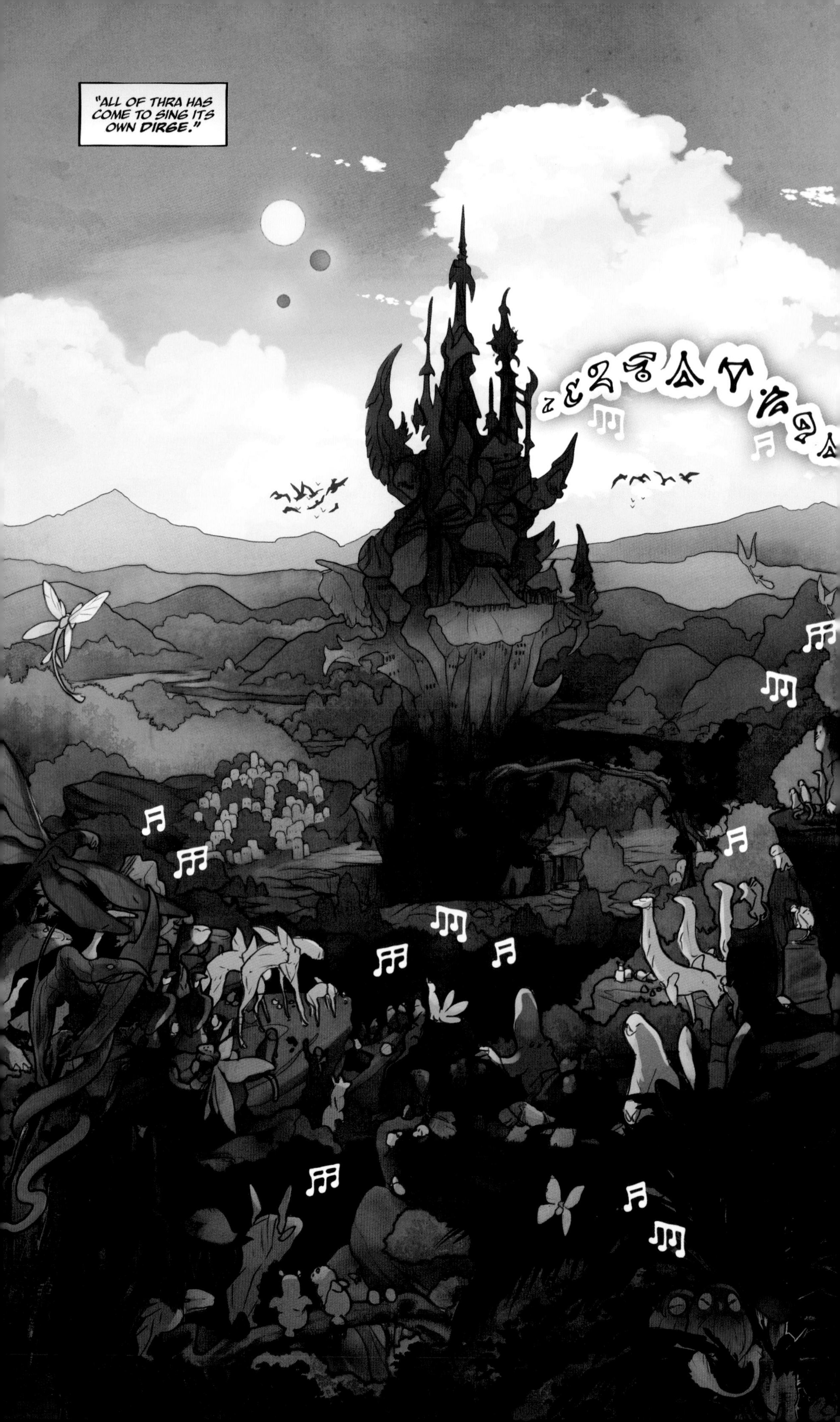
"ALL OF THRA HAS COME TO SING ITS OWN DIRGE."

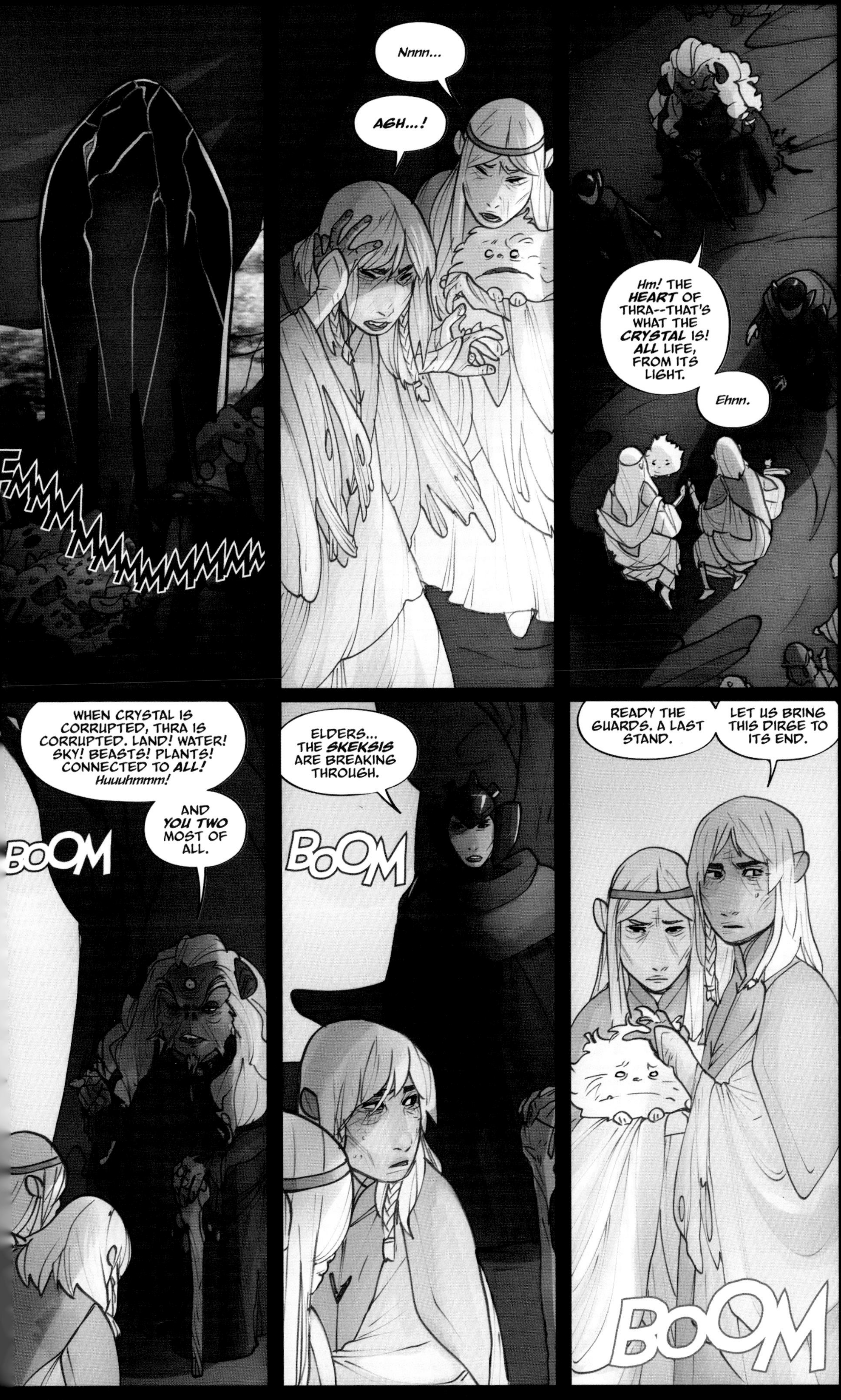
FMMMMMMMMMMMMMM
Nnnn...
AGH...!
Hm! The heart of Thra--that's what the crystal is! All life, from its light.
Ehnn.
When crystal is corrupted, Thra is corrupted. Land! Water! Sky! Beasts! Plants! Connected to all! Huuuhmmm!
And you two most of all.
BOOM
Elders... the Skeksis are breaking through.
BOOM
Ready the guards. A last stand.
Let us bring this dirge to its end.
BOOM

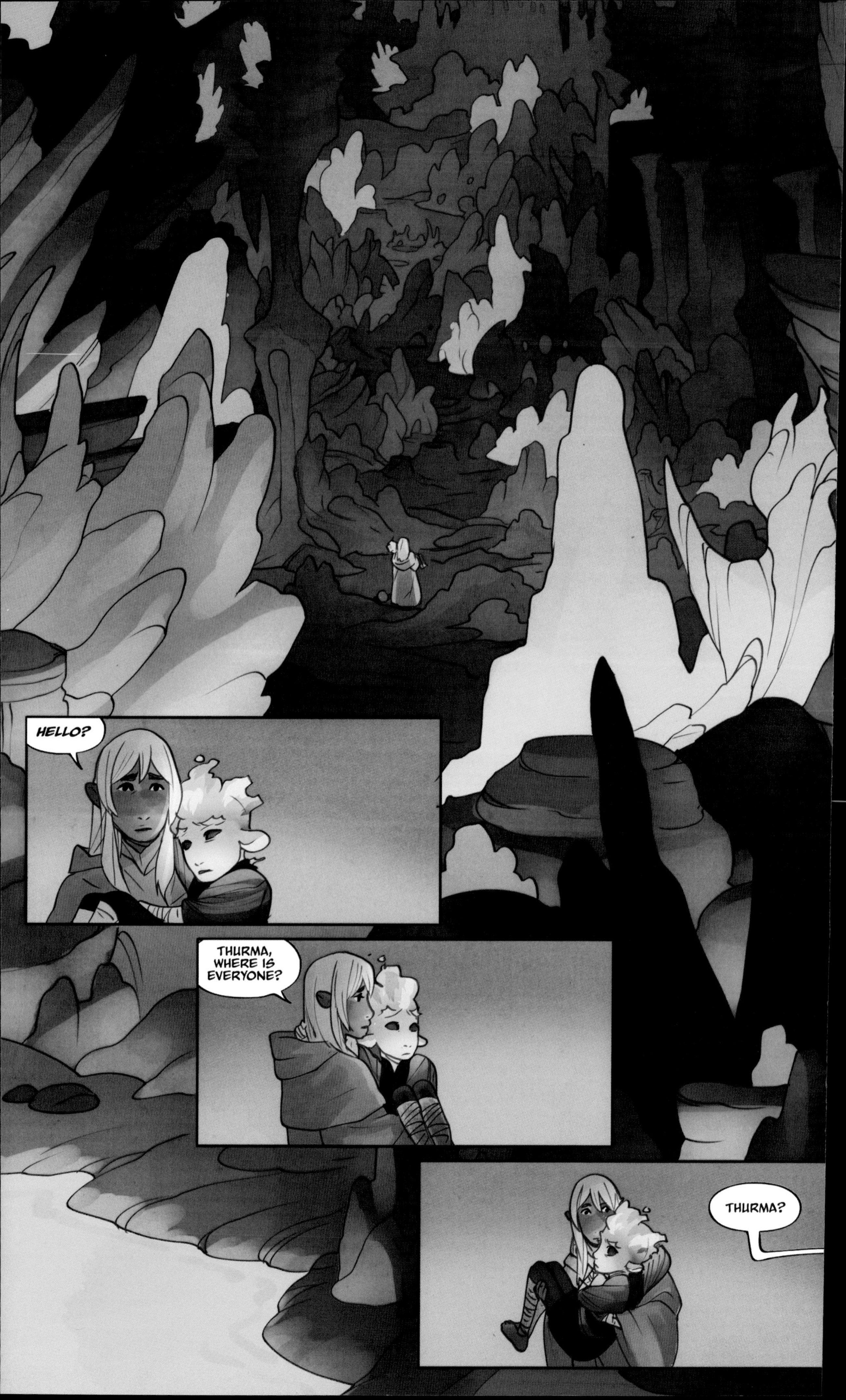
HELLO?
THURMA, WHERE IS EVERYONE?
THURMA?

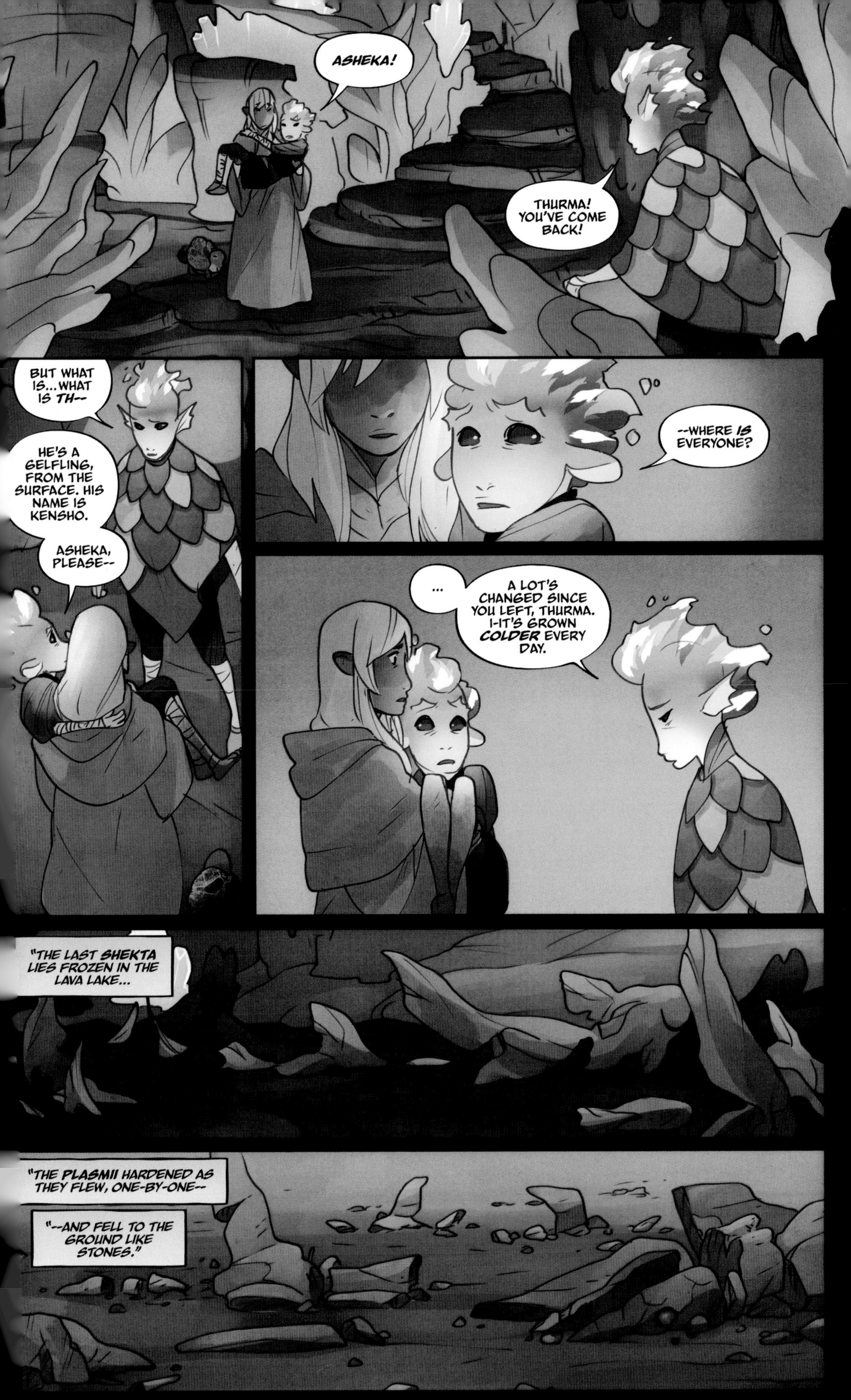
ASHEKA!
THURMA! YOU'VE COME BACK!
BUT WHAT IS...WHAT IS TH--
--WHERE IS EVERYONE?
HE'S A GELFLING, FROM THE SURFACE. HIS NAME IS KENSHO.
ASHEKA, PLEASE--
...
A LOT'S CHANGED SINCE YOU LEFT, THURMA. I-IT'S GROWN COLDER EVERY DAY.
"THE LAST SHEKTA LIES FROZEN IN THE LAVA LAKE...
"THE PLASMII HARDENED AS THEY FLEW, ONE-BY-ONE--
"--AND FELL TO THE GROUND LIKE STONES."

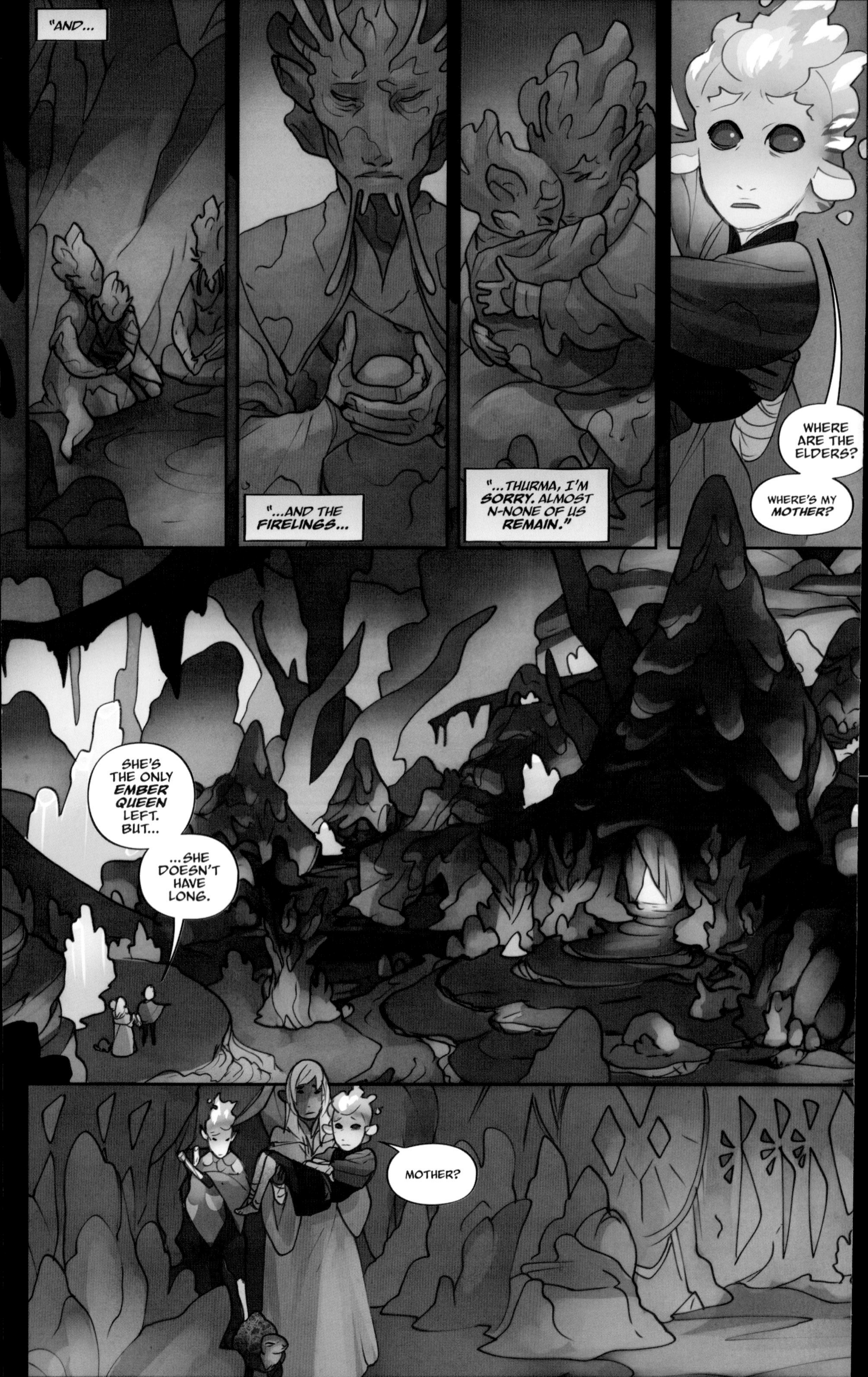
"AND...
"...AND THE FIRELINGS...
"...THURMA, I'M SORRY. ALMOST N-NONE OF US REMAIN."
WHERE ARE THE ELDERS?
WHERE'S MY MOTHER?
SHE'S THE ONLY EMBER QUEEN LEFT. BUT...
...SHE DOESN'T HAVE LONG.
MOTHER?

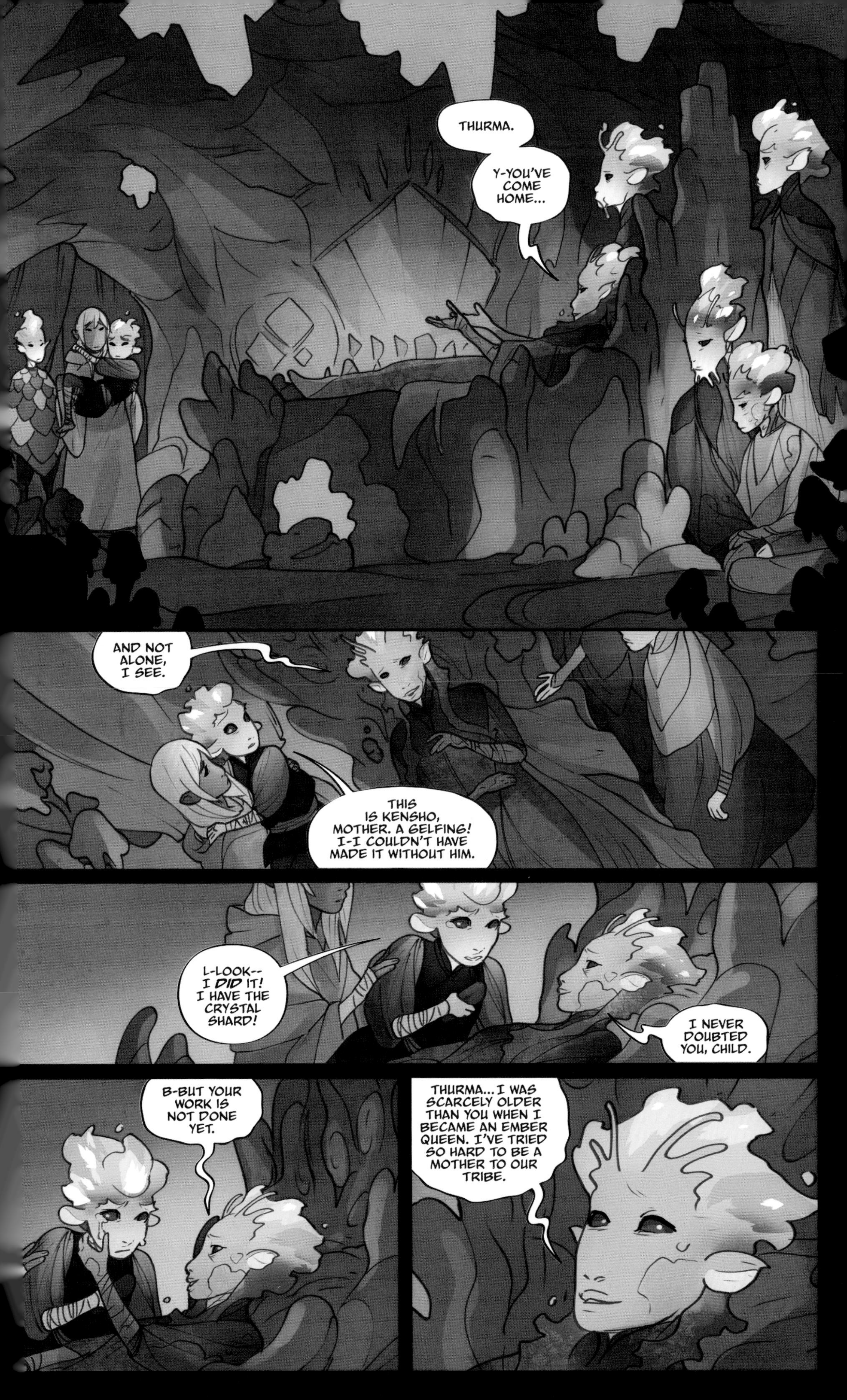
THURMA.
Y-YOU'VE COME HOME...
AND NOT ALONE, I SEE.
THIS IS KENSHO, MOTHER. A GELFING! I-I COULDN'T HAVE MADE IT WITHOUT HIM.
L-LOOK-- I *DID* IT! I HAVE THE CRYSTAL SHARD!
I NEVER DOUBTED YOU, CHILD.
B-BUT YOUR WORK IS NOT DONE YET.
THURMA... I WAS SCARCELY OLDER THAN YOU WHEN I BECAME AN EMBER QUEEN. I'VE TRIED SO HARD TO BE A MOTHER TO OUR TRIBE.

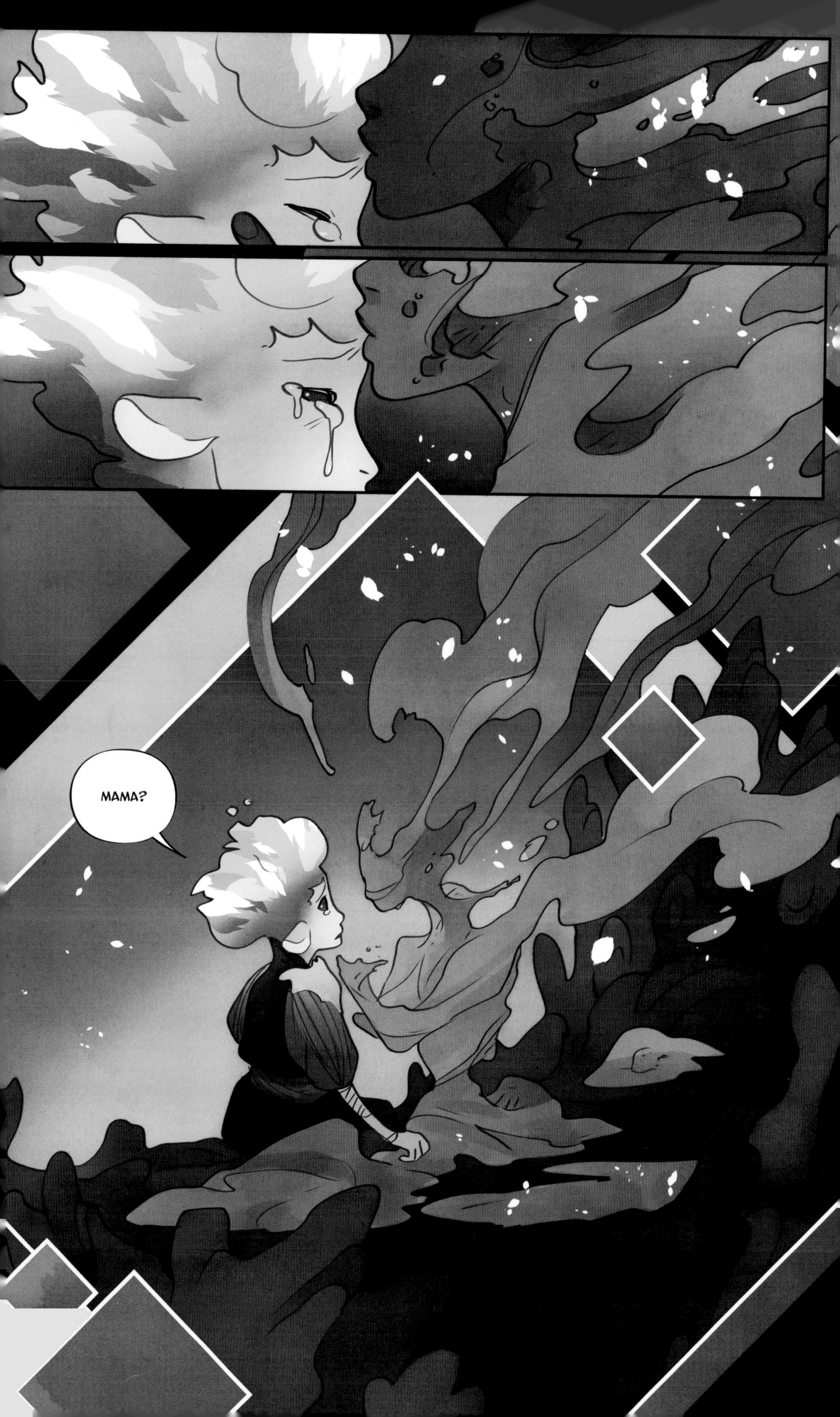
MAMA?

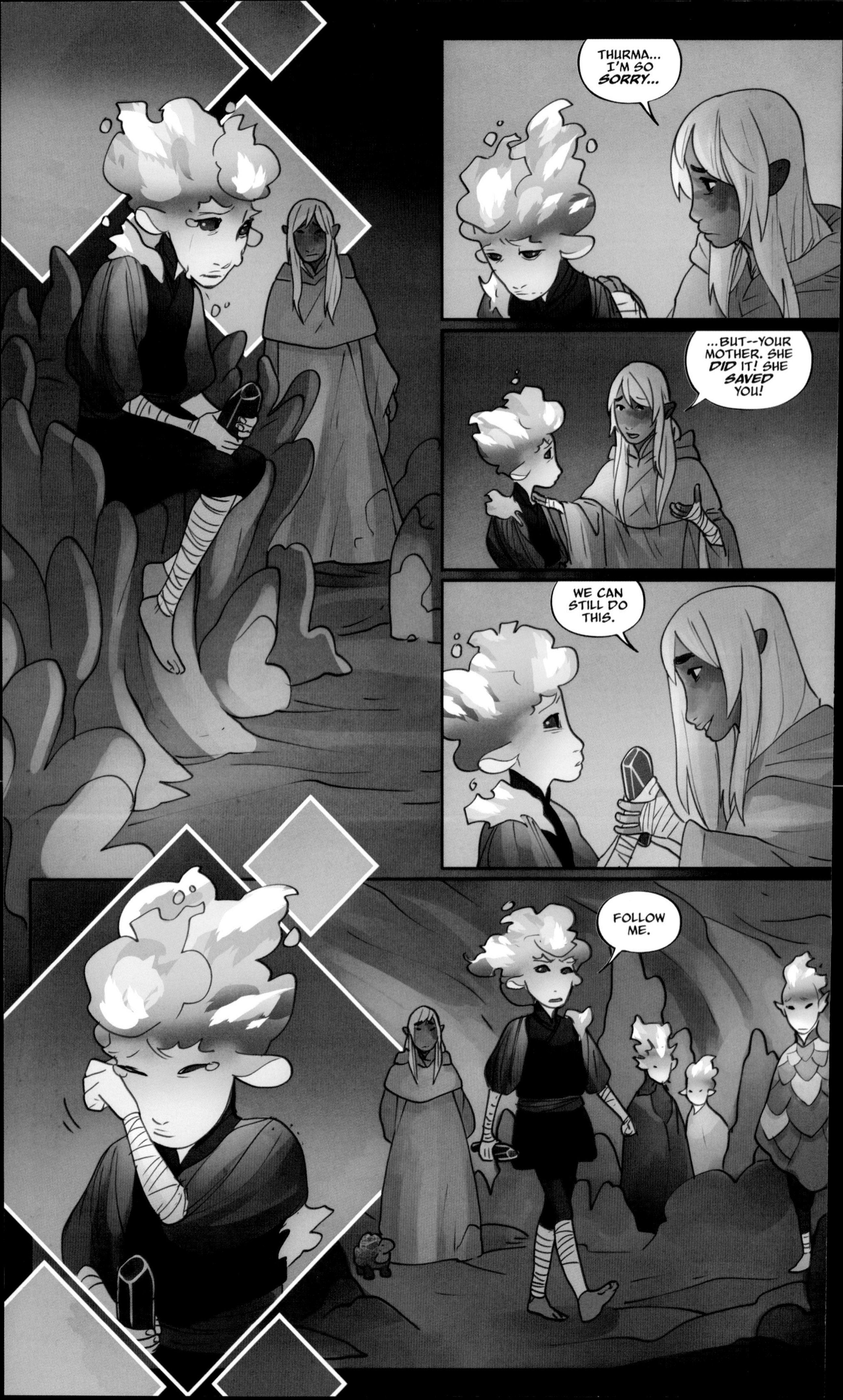
THURMA... I'M SO SORRY...
...BUT--YOUR MOTHER. SHE DID IT! SHE SAVED YOU!
WE CAN STILL DO THIS.
FOLLOW ME.

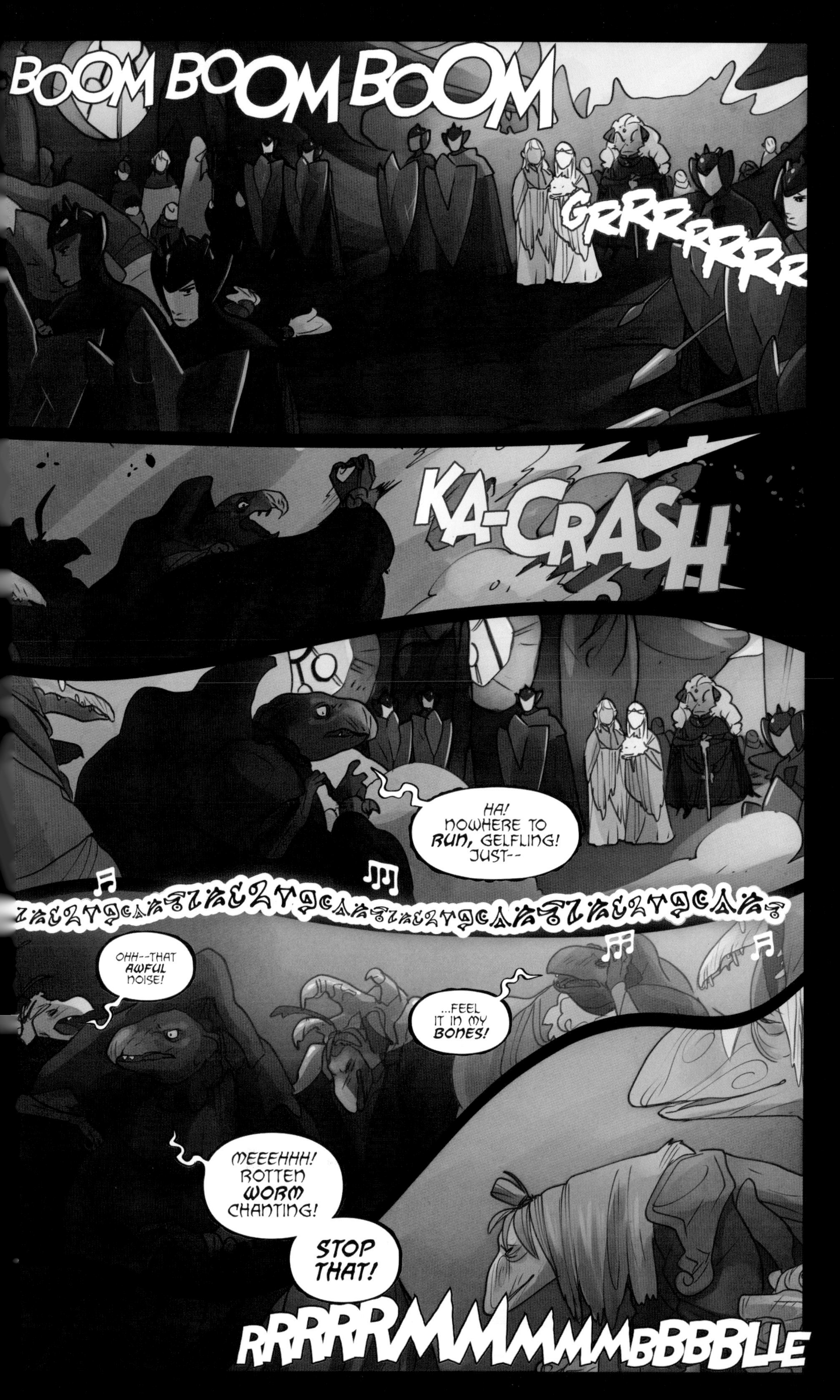
BOOM BOOM BOOM
GRRRRRRRR
KA-CRASH
HA! NOWHERE TO RUN, GELFLING! JUST--
OHH--THAT AWFUL NOISE!
...FEEL IT IN MY BONES!
MEEEHHH! ROTTEN WORM CHANTING!
STOP THAT!
RRRRRMMMMMMBBBBLLE

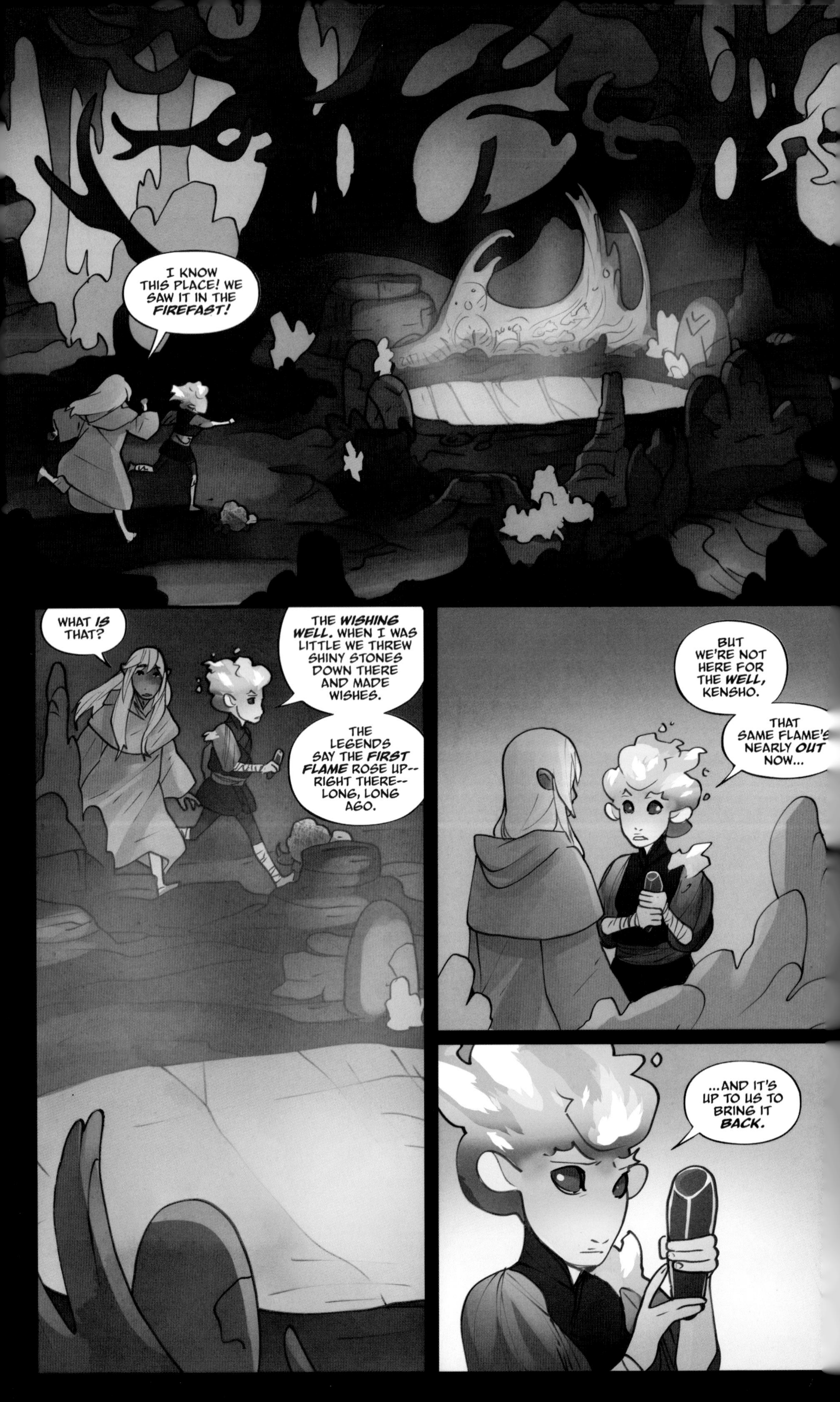
I KNOW THIS PLACE! WE SAW IT IN THE FIREFAST!
WHAT IS THAT?
THE WISHING WELL. WHEN I WAS LITTLE WE THREW SHINY STONES DOWN THERE AND MADE WISHES.
THE LEGENDS SAY THE FIRST FLAME ROSE UP-- RIGHT THERE-- LONG, LONG AGO.
BUT WE'RE NOT HERE FOR THE WELL, KENSHO.
THAT SAME FLAME'S NEARLY OUT NOW...
...AND IT'S UP TO US TO BRING IT BACK.

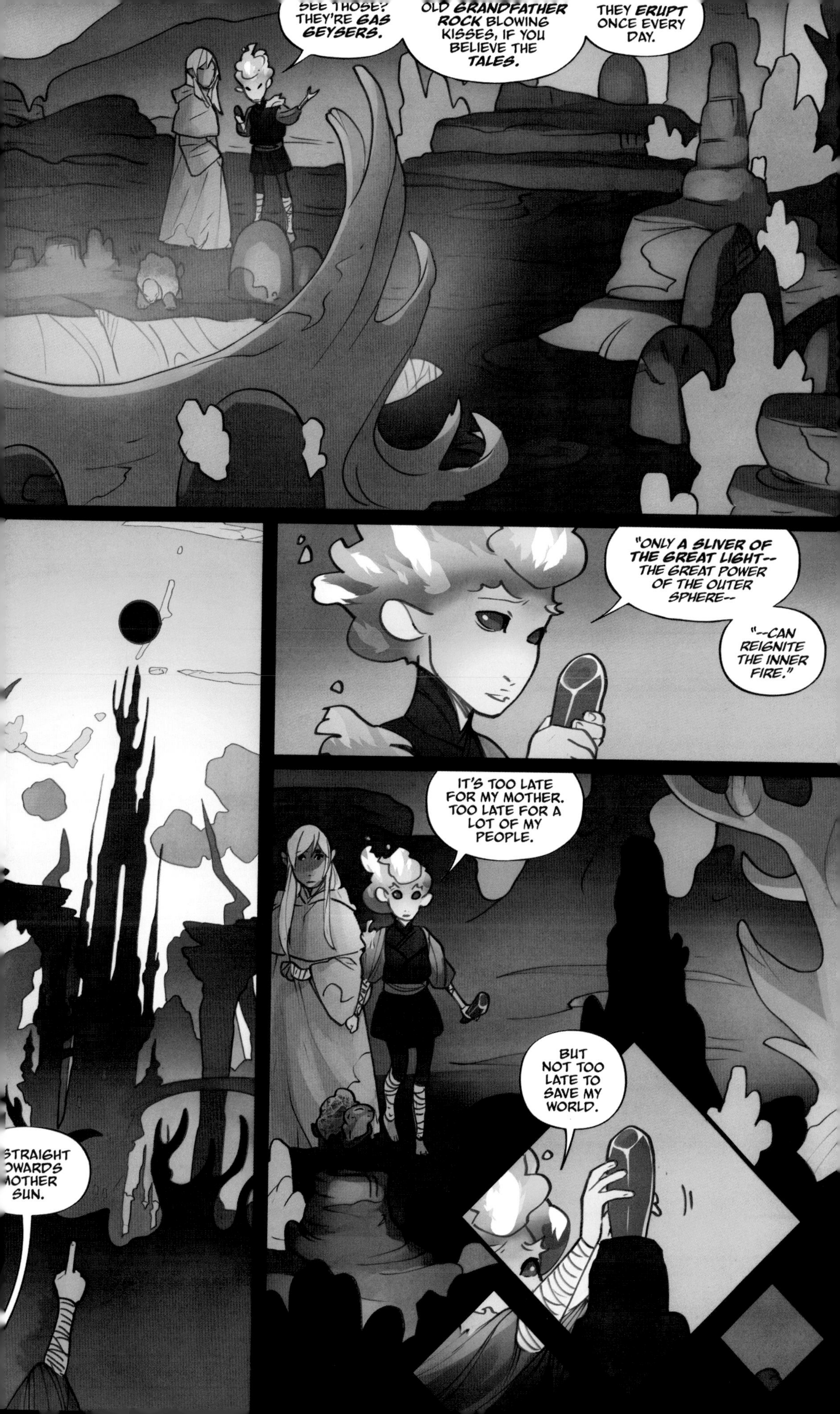
SEE THOSE? THEY'RE GAS GEYSERS.
OLD GRANDFATHER ROCK BLOWING KISSES, IF YOU BELIEVE THE TALES.
THEY ERUPT ONCE EVERY DAY.
STRAIGHT TOWARDS MOTHER SUN.
"ONLY A SLIVER OF THE GREAT LIGHT-- THE GREAT POWER OF THE OUTER SPHERE--
"--CAN REIGNITE THE INNER FIRE."
IT'S TOO LATE FOR MY MOTHER. TOO LATE FOR A LOT OF MY PEOPLE.
BUT NOT TOO LATE TO SAVE MY WORLD.

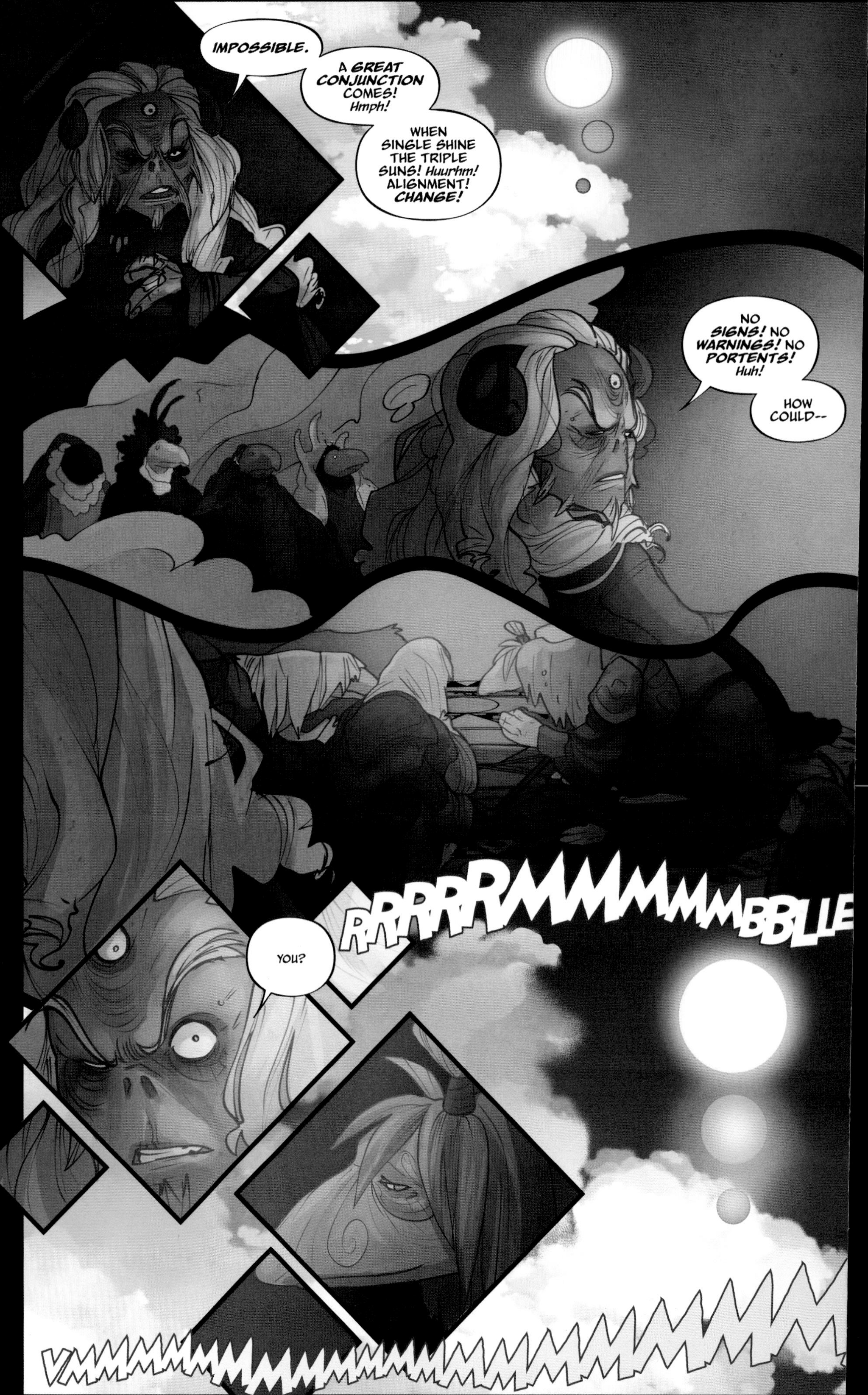
IMPOSSIBLE.
A GREAT CONJUNCTION COMES! Hmph!
WHEN SINGLE SHINE THE TRIPLE SUNS! Huurhm! ALIGNMENT! CHANGE!
NO SIGNS! NO WARNINGS! NO PORTENTS! Huh!
HOW COULD--
RRRRRMMMMMMMBBLLE
YOU?
VMMMMMMMMMMMMMMMMMMMMMMMMMMM

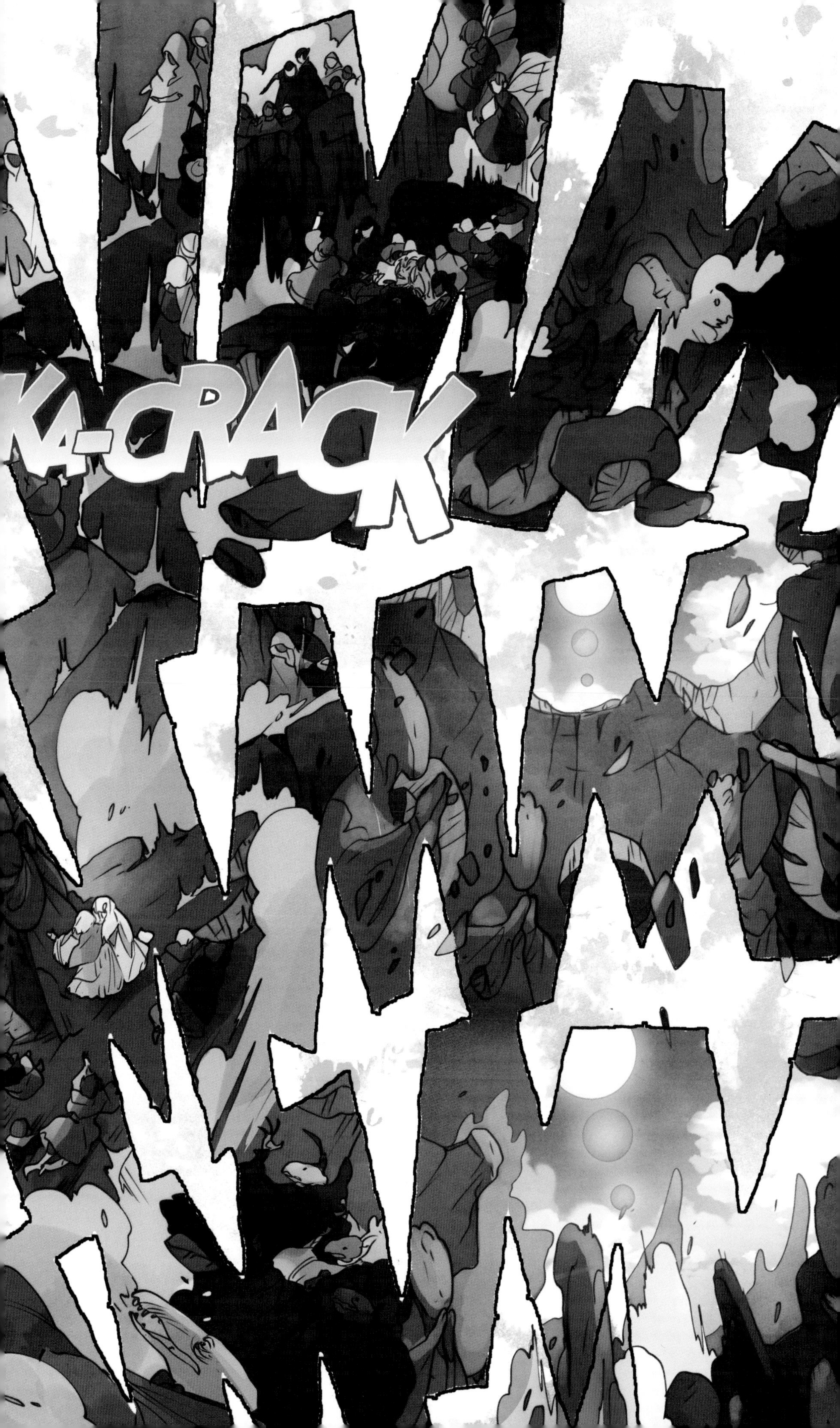
KA-CRACK

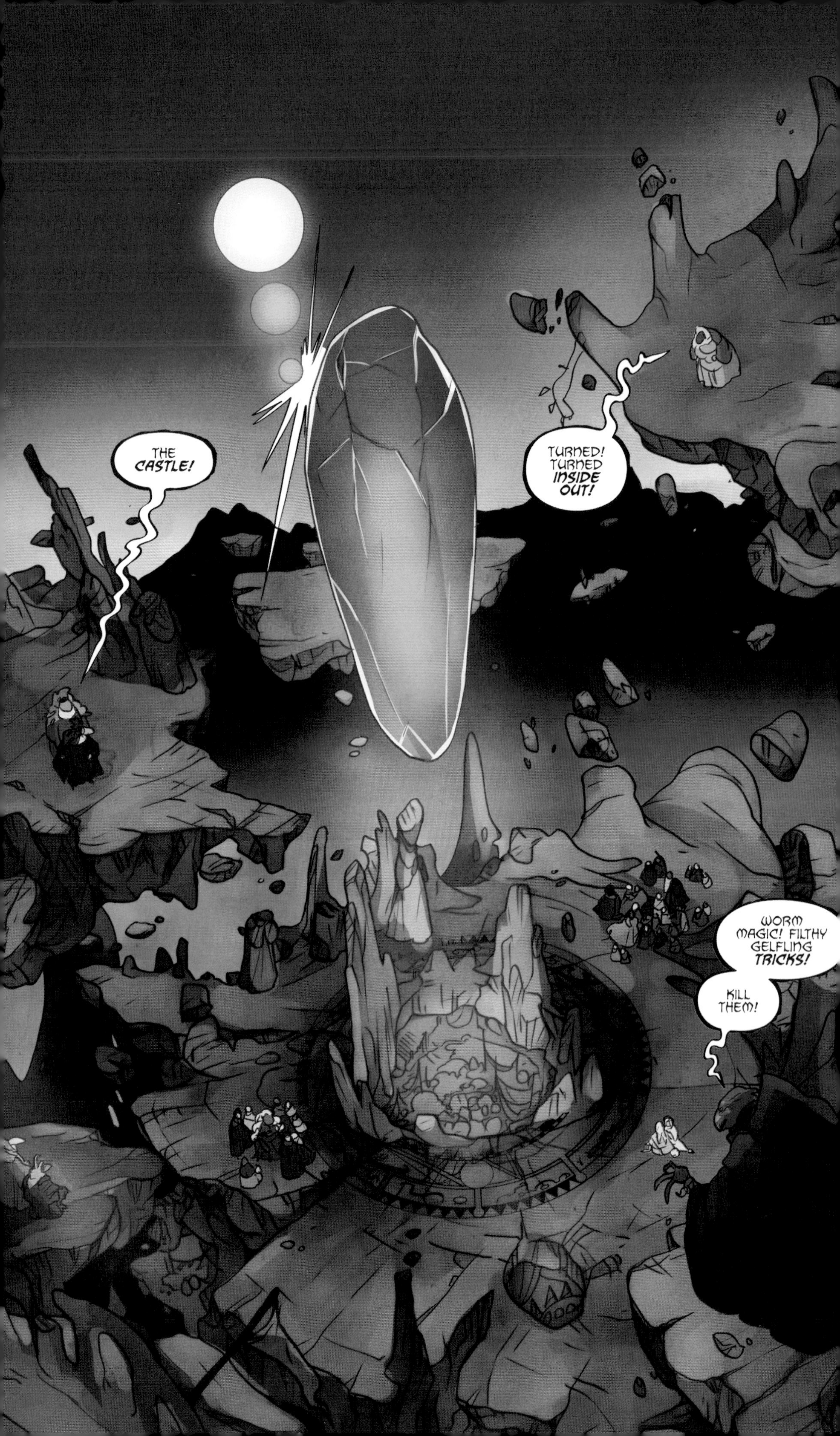
THE CASTLE!
TURNED! TURNED INSIDE OUT!
WORM MAGIC! FILTHY GELFLING TRICKS!
KILL THEM!

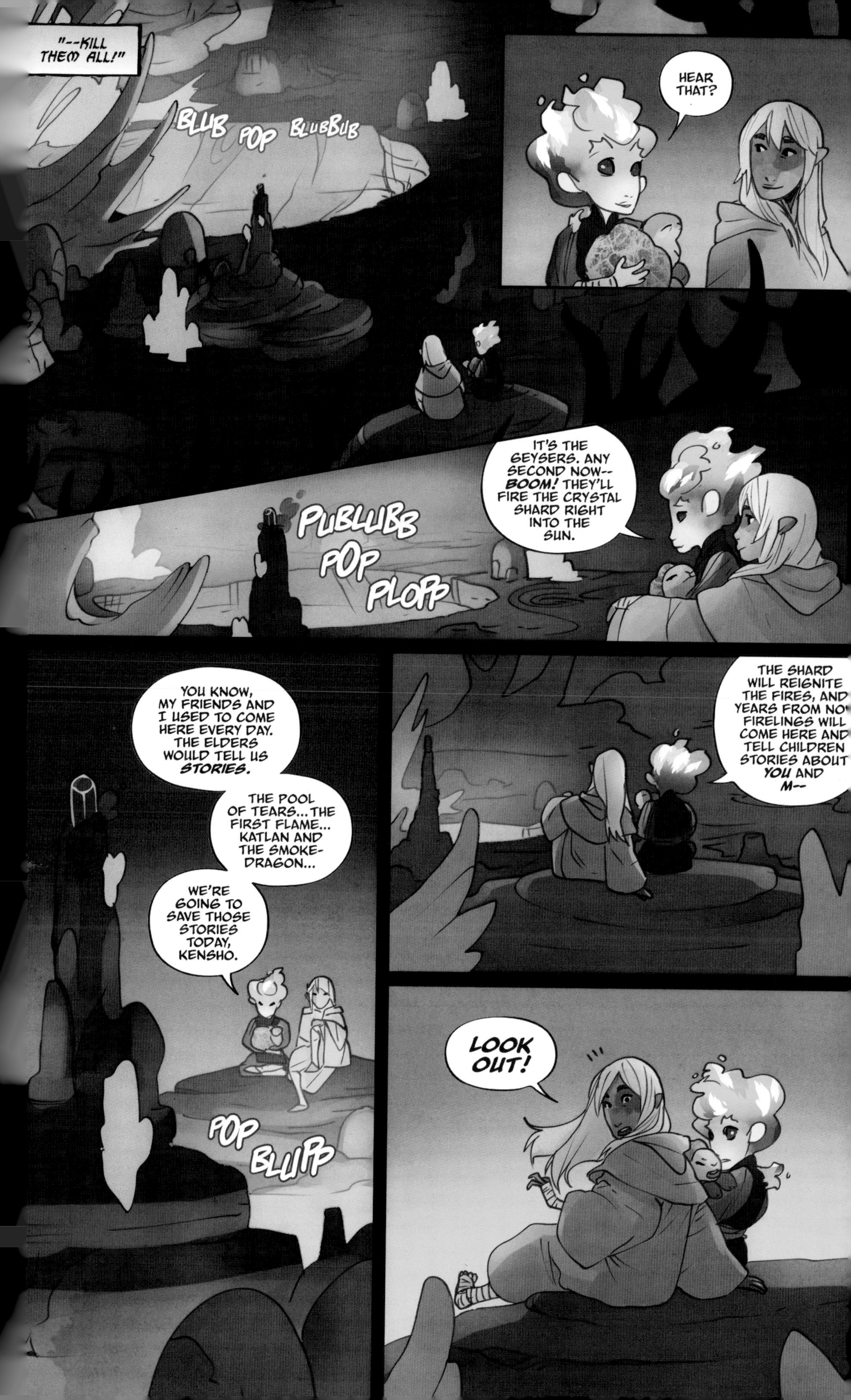
"--KILL THEM ALL!"
BLUB POP BLUBBUB
HEAR THAT?
IT'S THE GEYSERS. ANY SECOND NOW-- BOOM! THEY'LL FIRE THE CRYSTAL SHARD RIGHT INTO THE SUN.
PUBLUBB POP PLOPP
YOU KNOW, MY FRIENDS AND I USED TO COME HERE EVERY DAY. THE ELDERS WOULD TELL US STORIES.
THE POOL OF TEARS...THE FIRST FLAME... KATLAN AND THE SMOKE-DRAGON...
WE'RE GOING TO SAVE THOSE STORIES TODAY, KENSHO.
POP BLUPP
THE SHARD WILL REIGNITE THE FIRES, AND YEARS FROM NO FIRELINGS WILL COME HERE AND TELL CHILDREN STORIES ABOUT YOU AND M--
LOOK OUT!

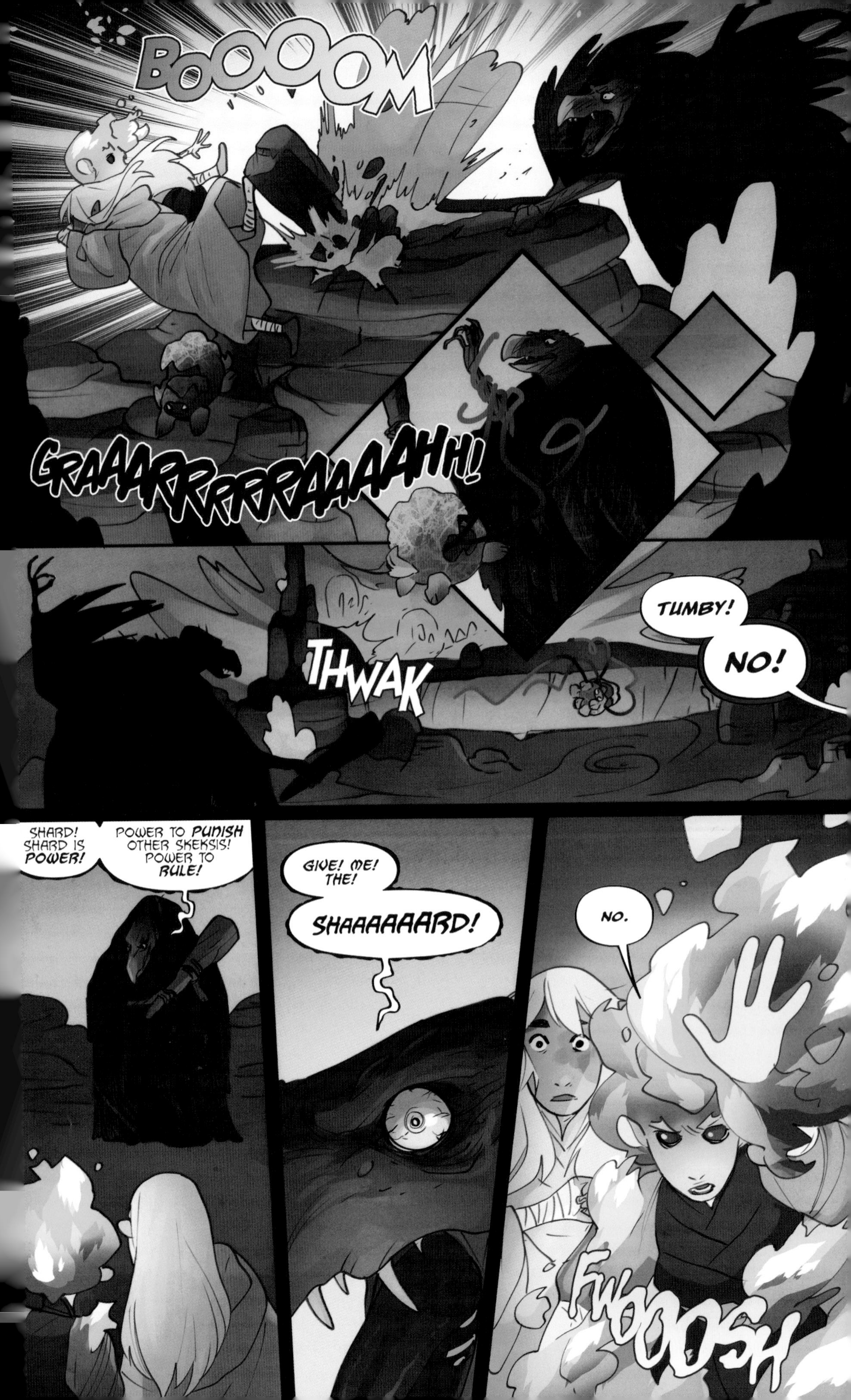
BOOOOOM
GRAAARRRRRRAAAAAHH!
THWAK
TUMBY!
NO!
SHARD! SHARD IS POWER!
POWER TO PUNISH OTHER SKEKSIS! POWER TO RULE!
GIVE! ME! THE!
SHAAAAAARD!
NO.
FWOOOSH

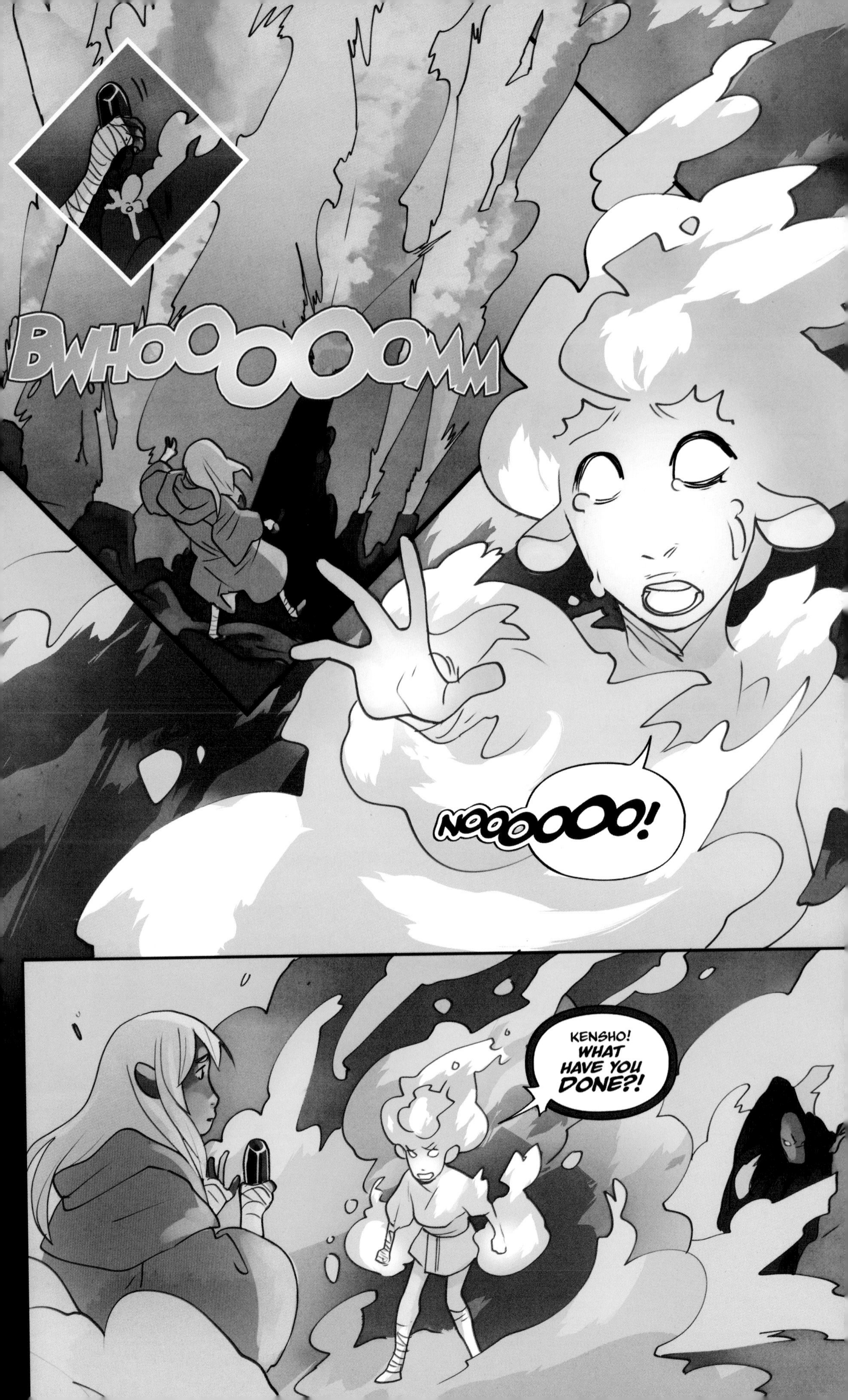
BWHOOOOOOMM
NOOOOOOO!
KENSHO! WHAT HAVE YOU DONE?!

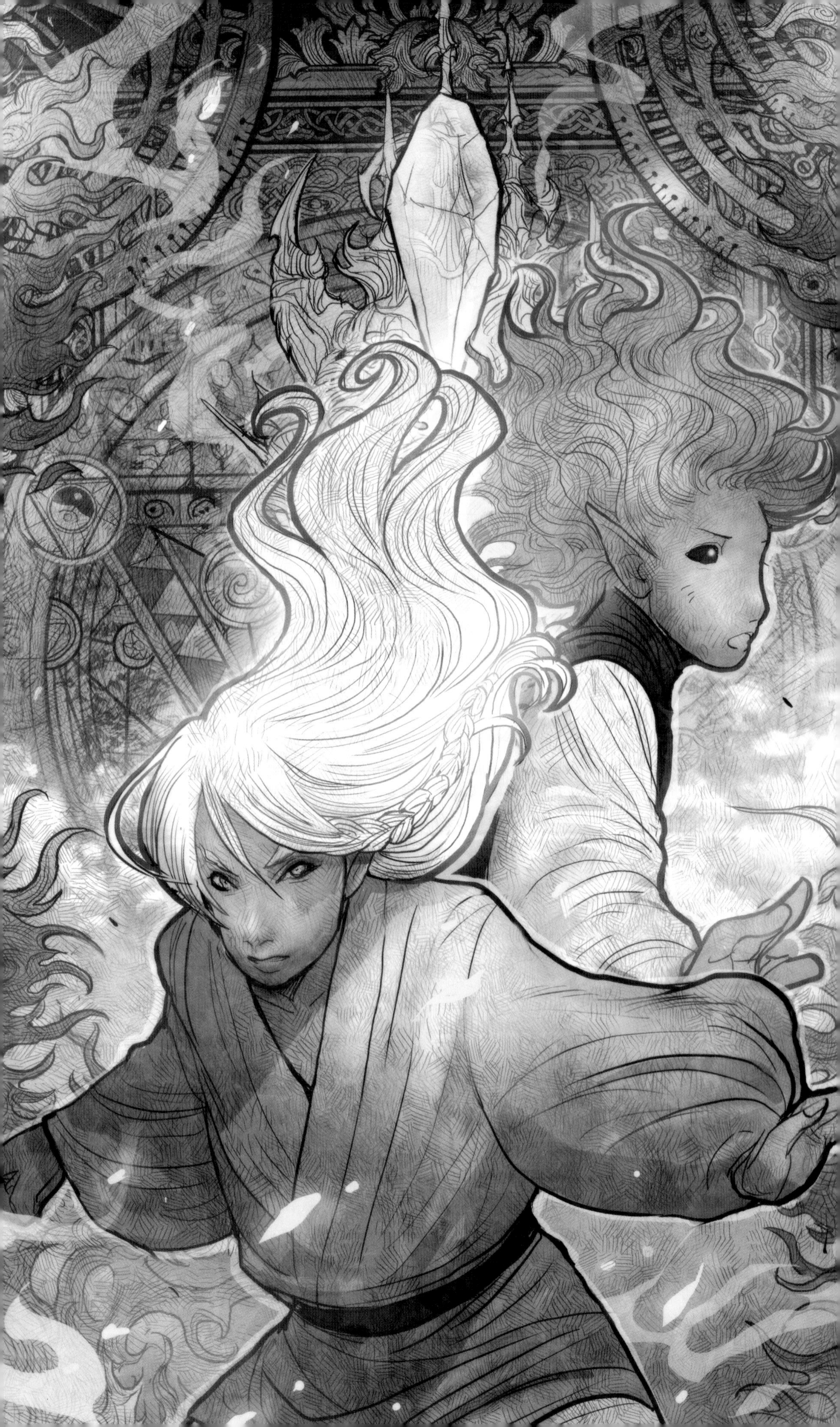

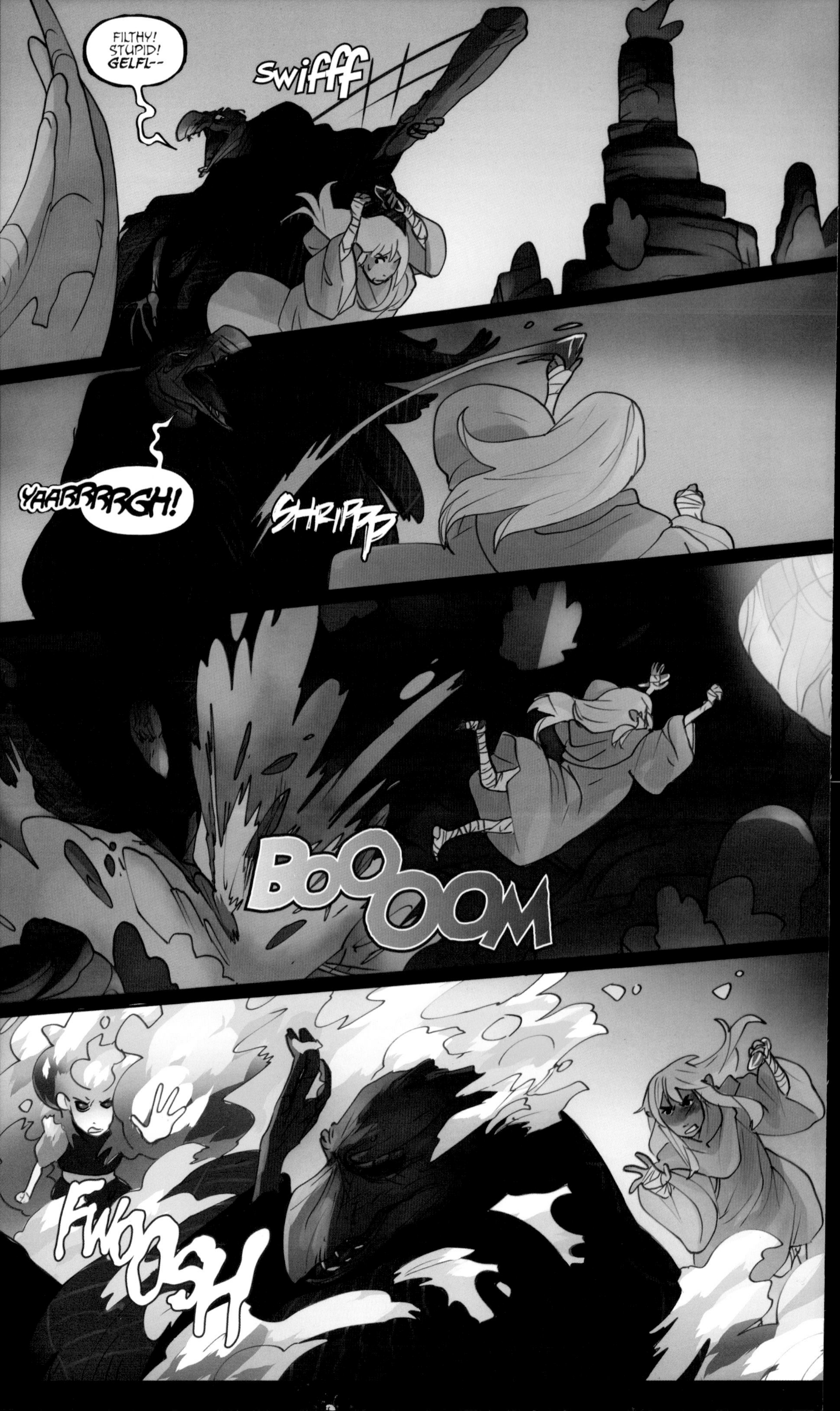
FILTHY! STUPID! GELFL--
SWIFFF
YAARRRRRGH!
SHRIPPP
BOOOOOM
FWOOSH

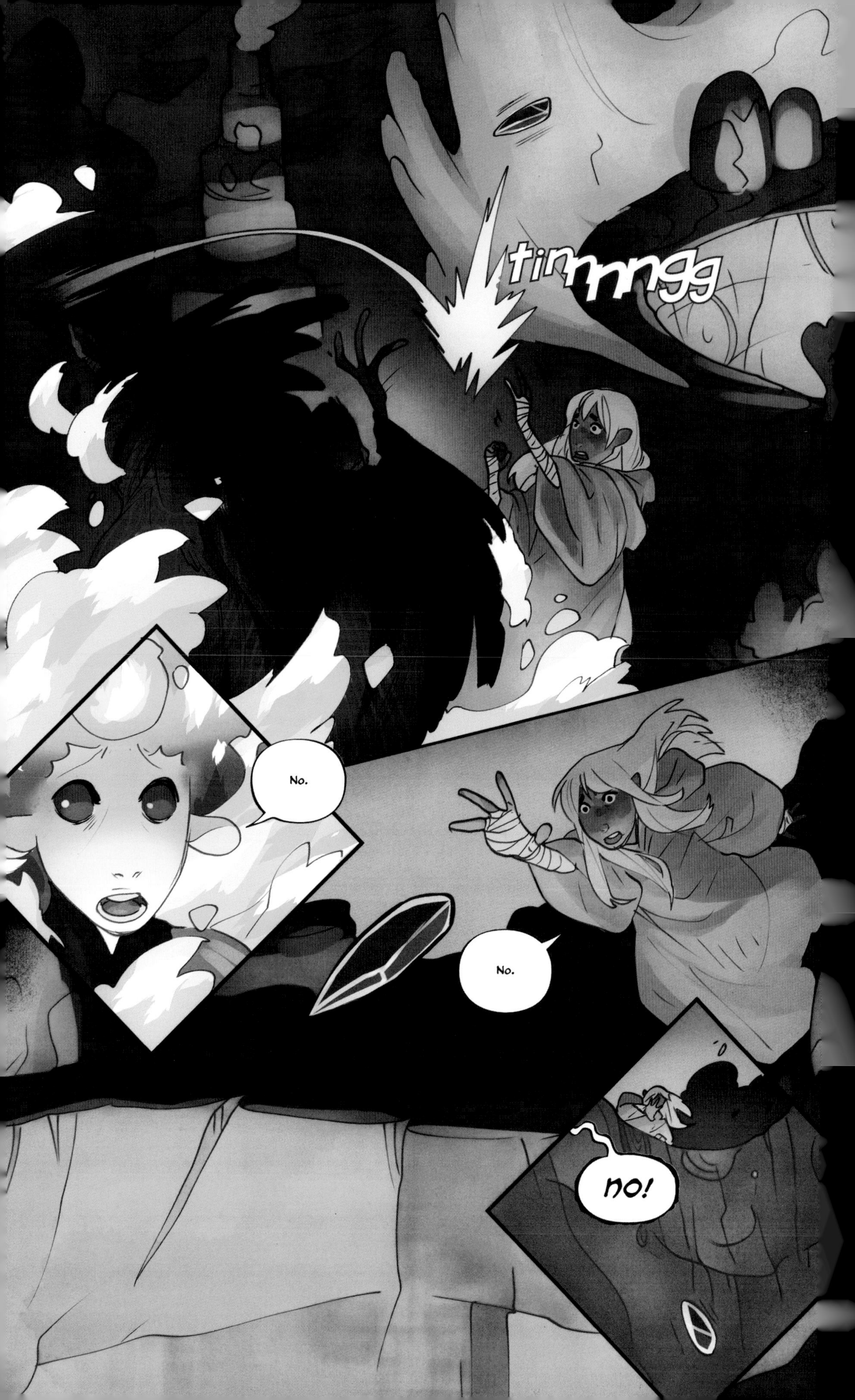
tinnnngg
No.
No.
no!

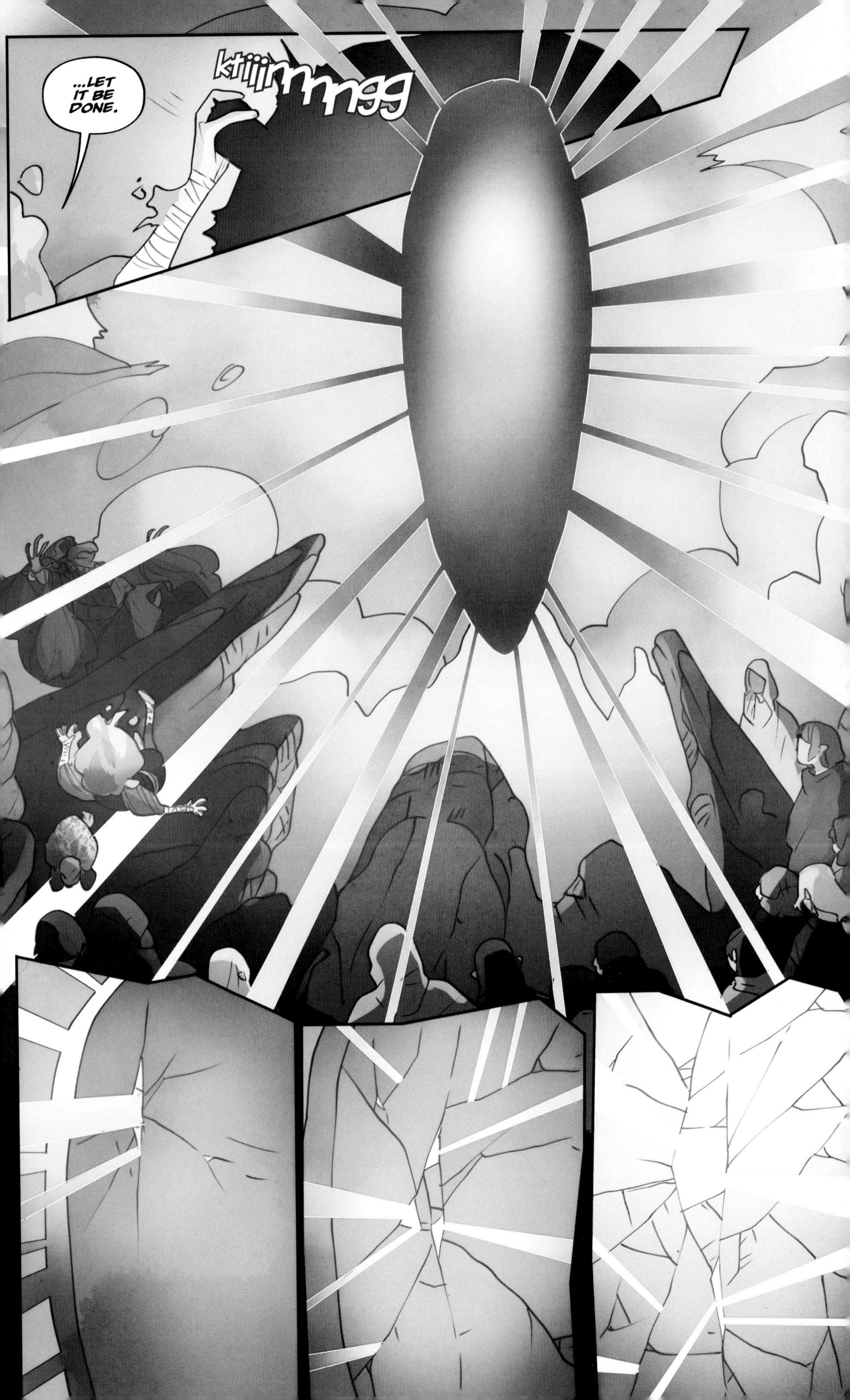
...LET IT BE DONE.
ktiiinnngg

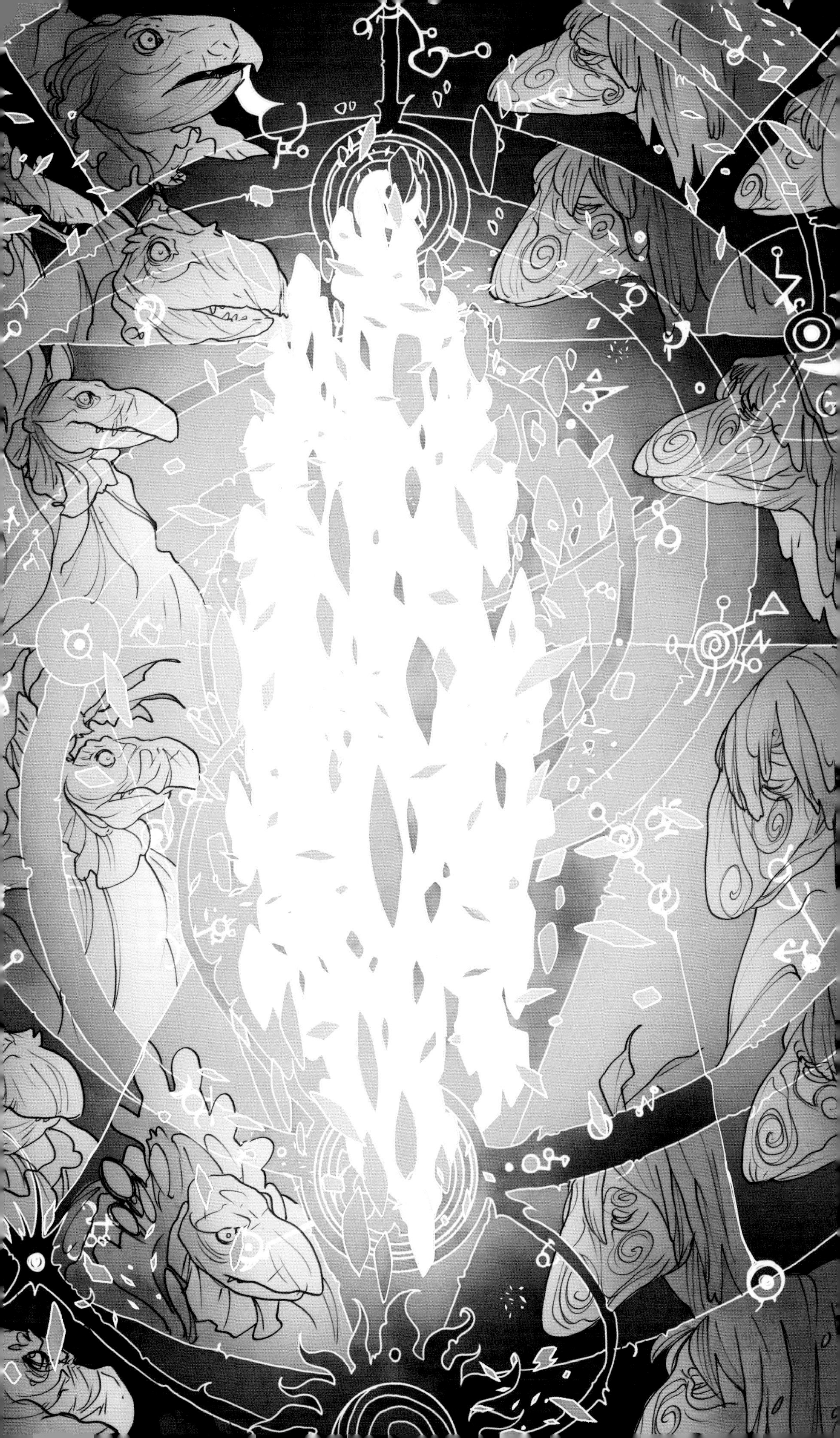

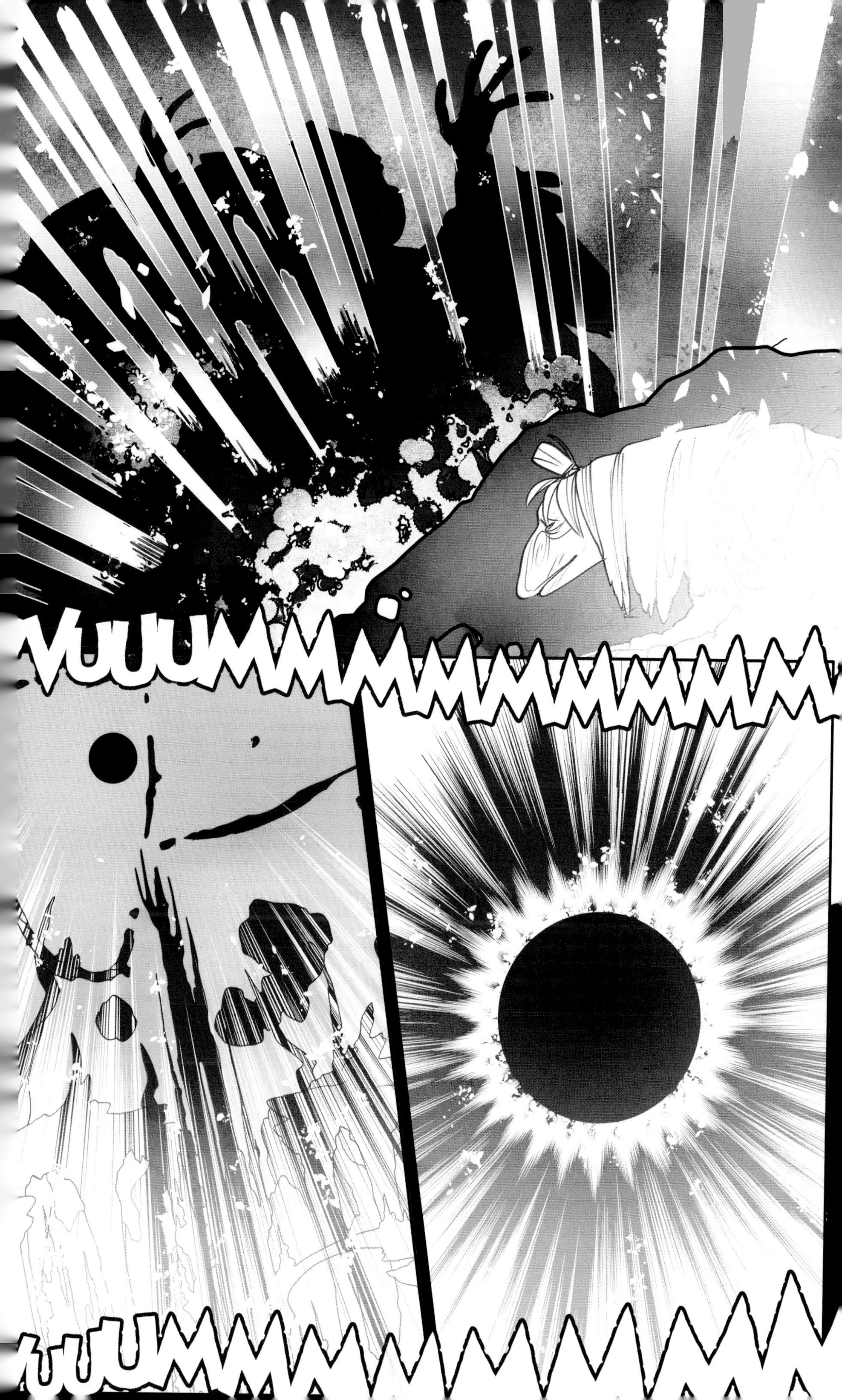
VUUUMMMMMMMMMMMMMMMM
UUMMMMMMMMMMMMM

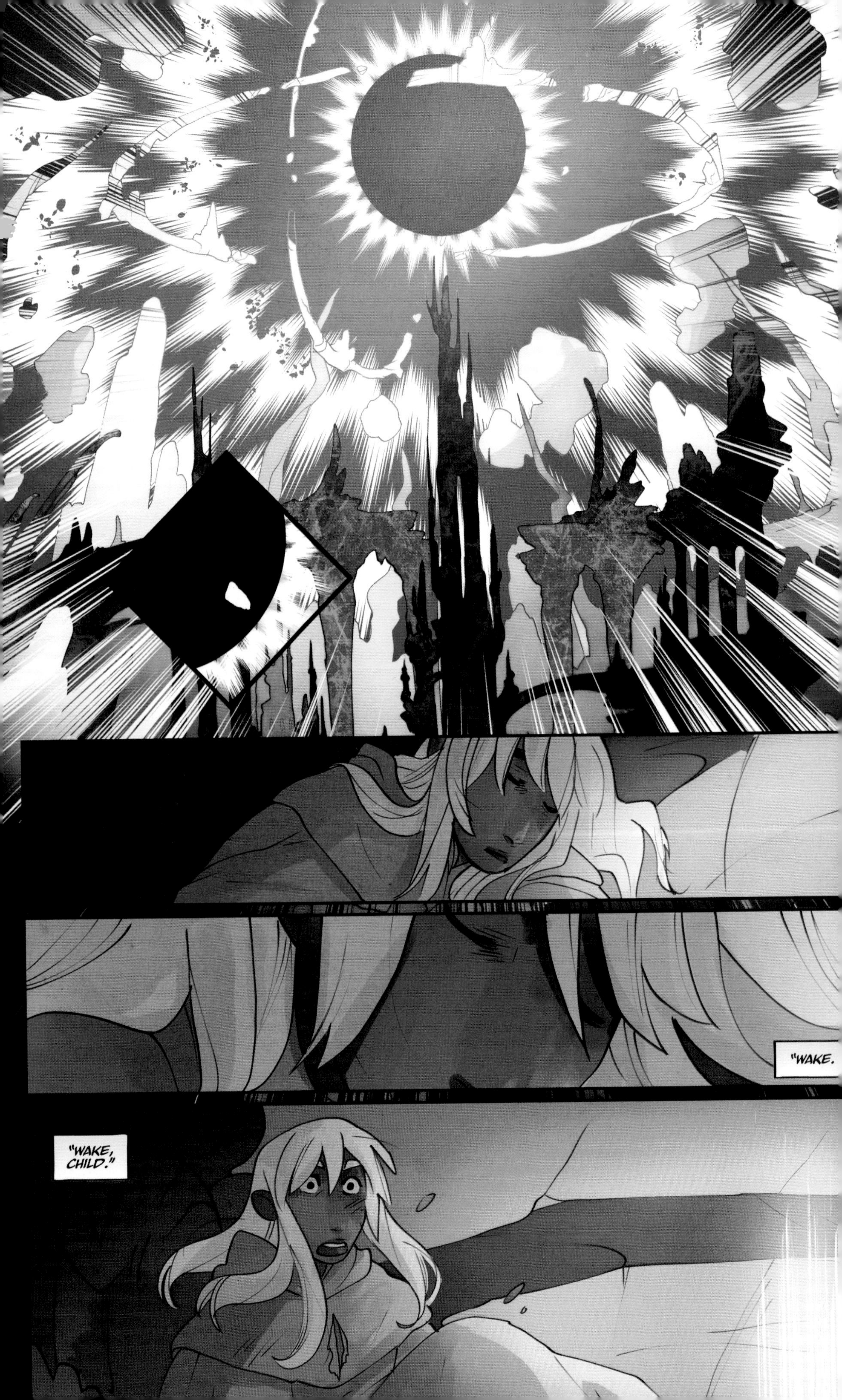
"WAKE.
"WAKE,
CHILD."

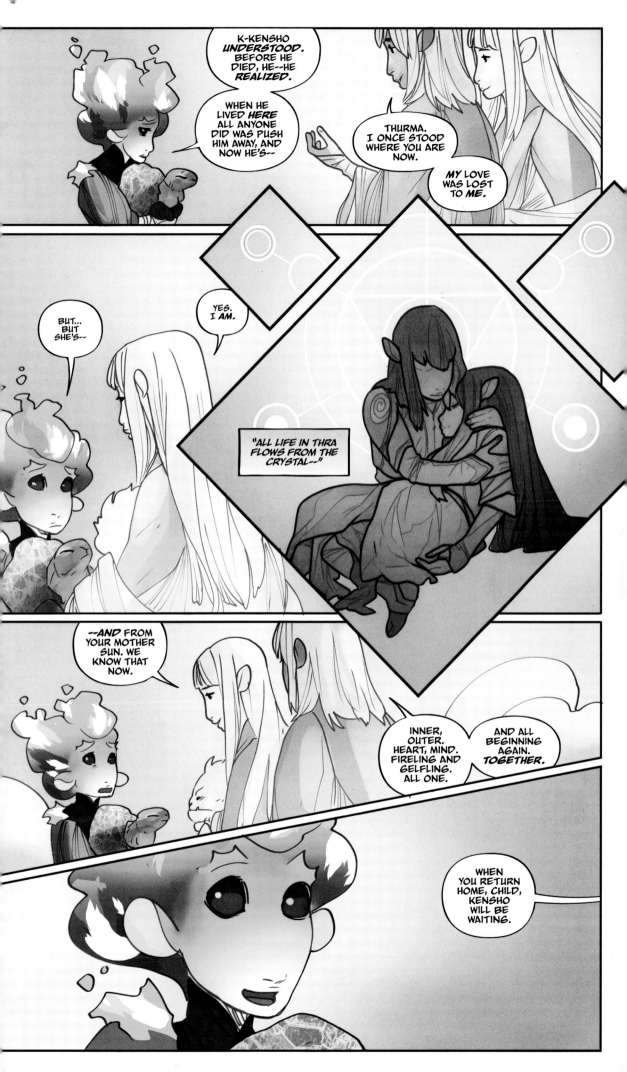

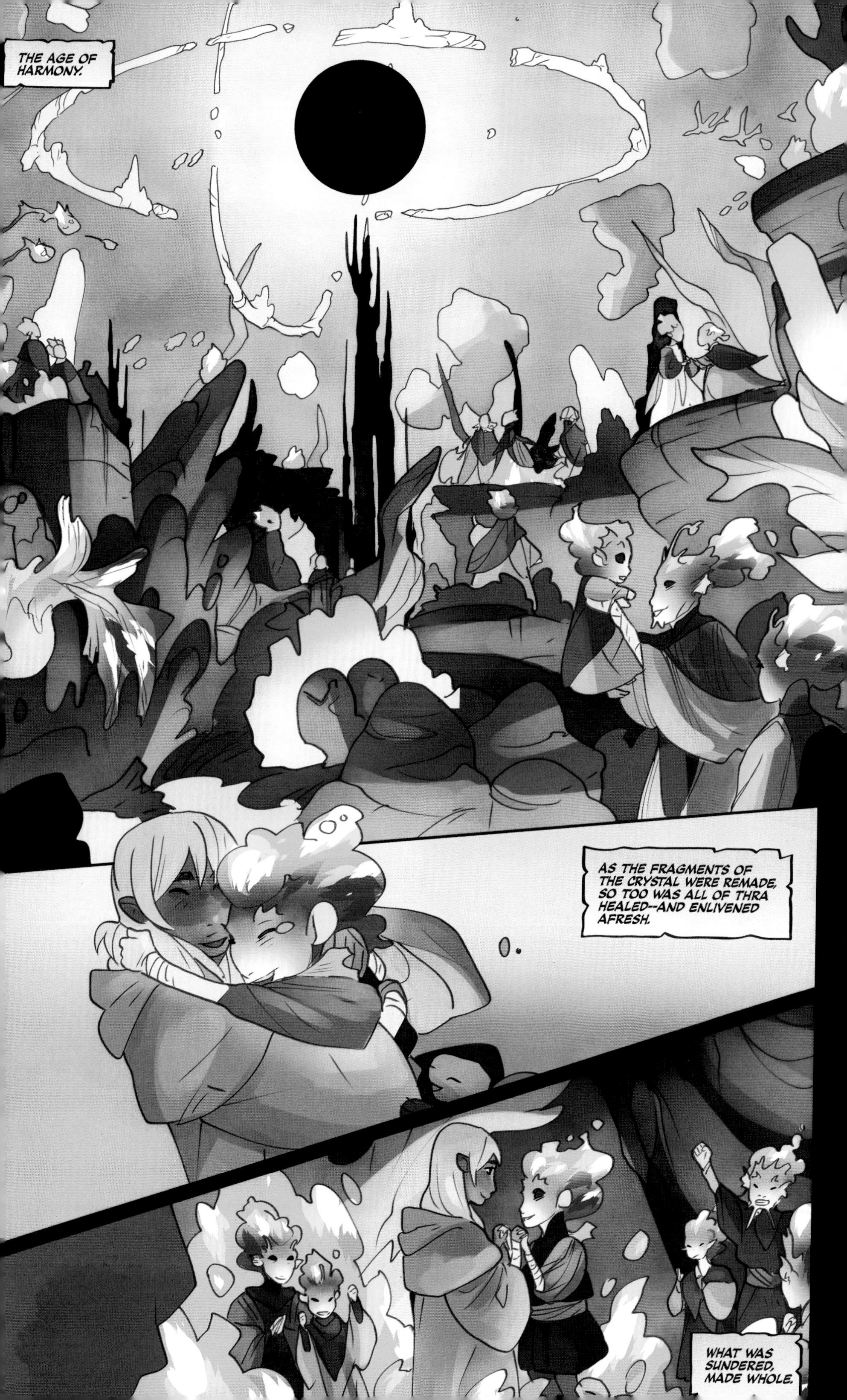
THE AGE OF HARMONY.
AS THE FRAGMENTS OF THE CRYSTAL WERE REMADE, SO TOO WAS ALL OF THRA HEALED--AND ENLIVENED AFRESH.
WHAT WAS SUNDERED, MADE WHOLE.

COVER
GALLERY

Facing page: Issue #9 Cover by Mark Buckingham.
Following pages: Issues #10-#12 Covers by Mark Buckingham

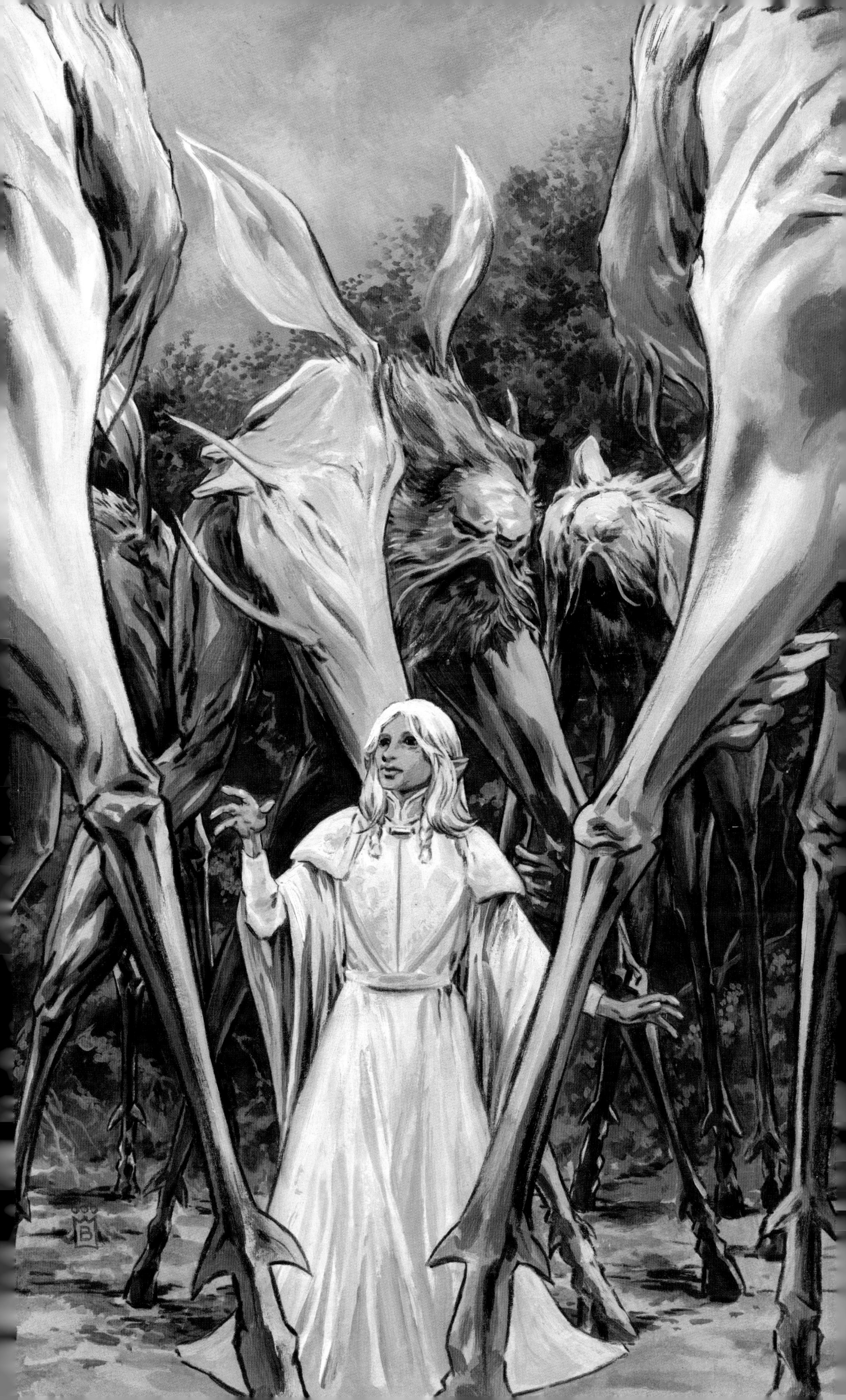

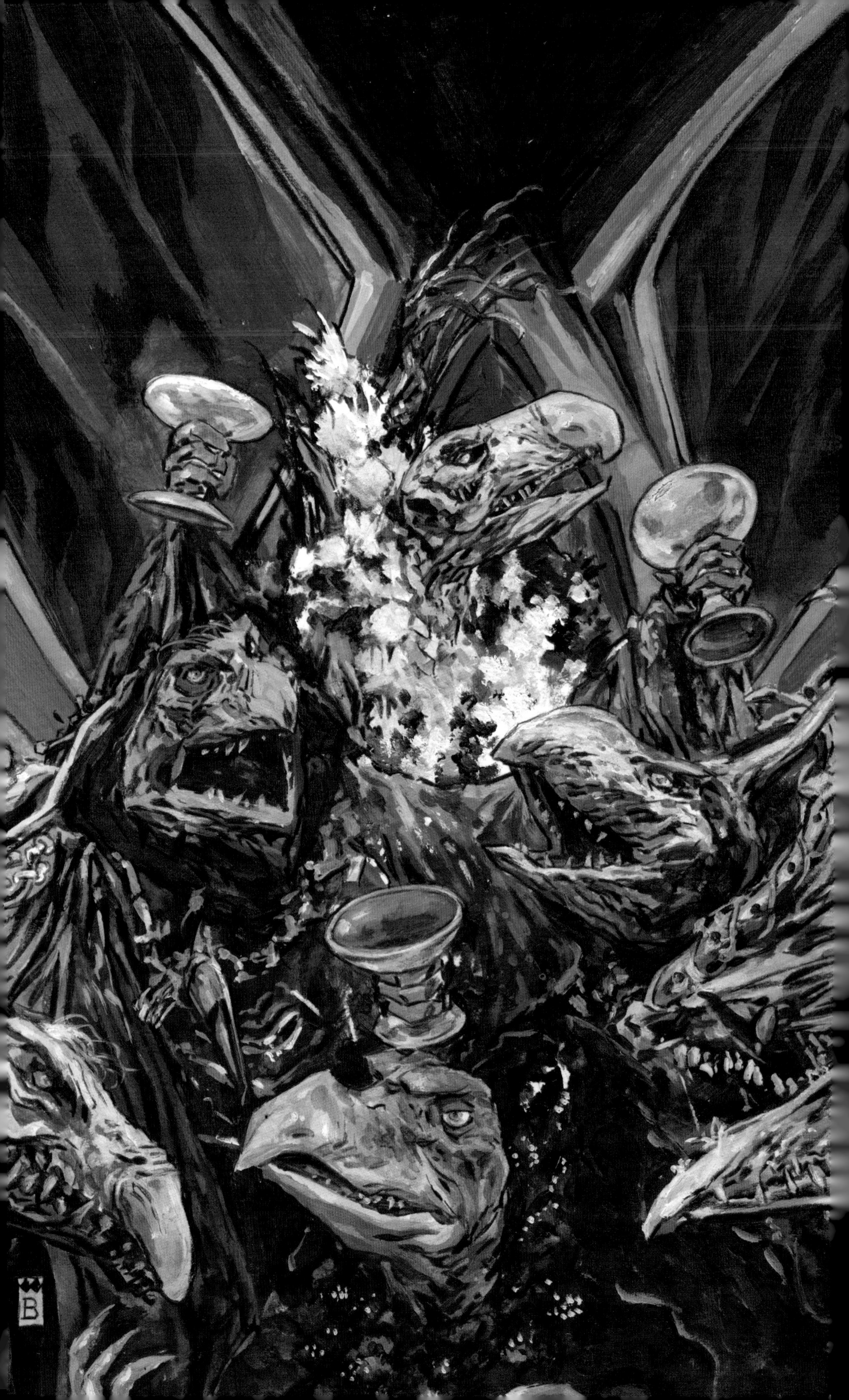

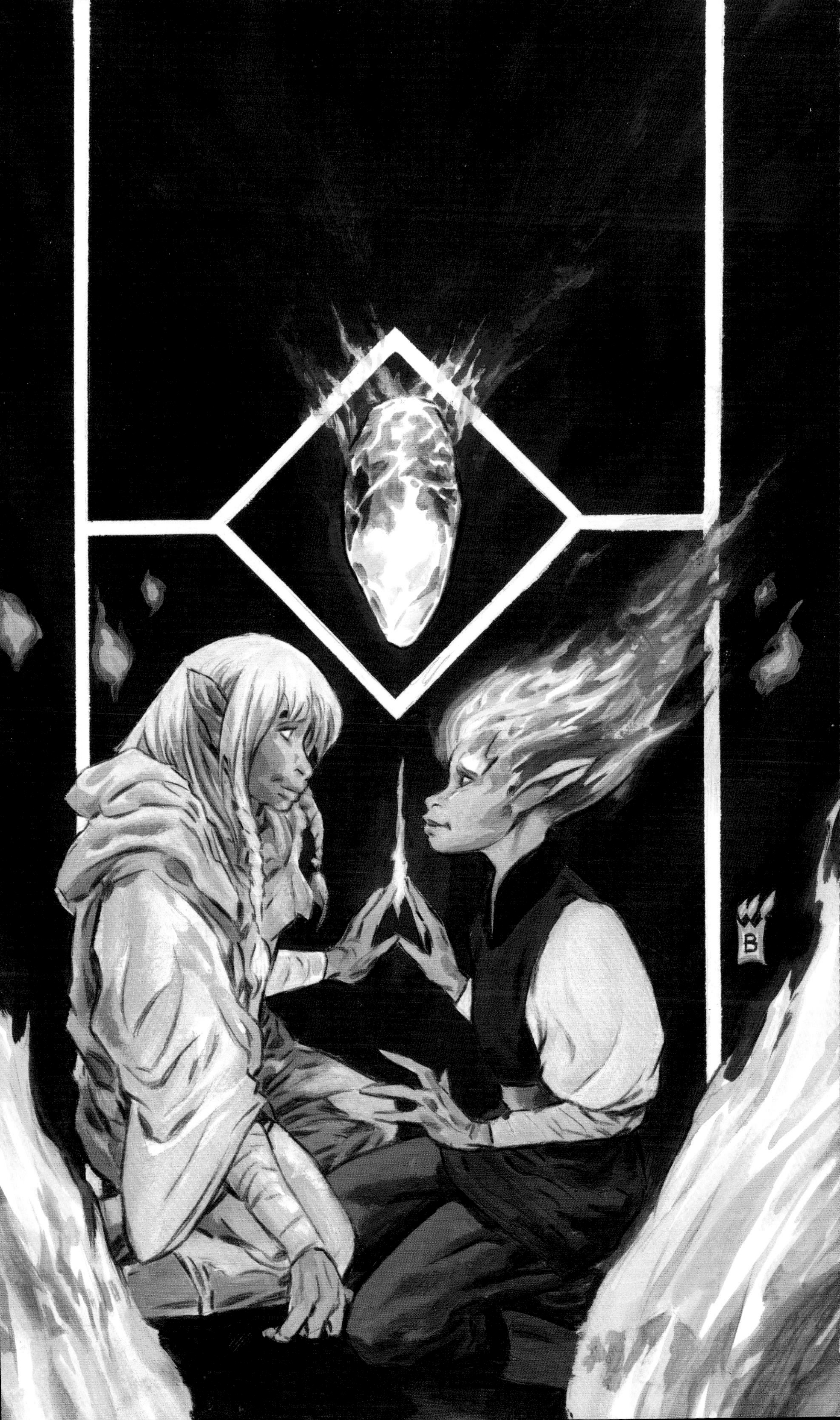

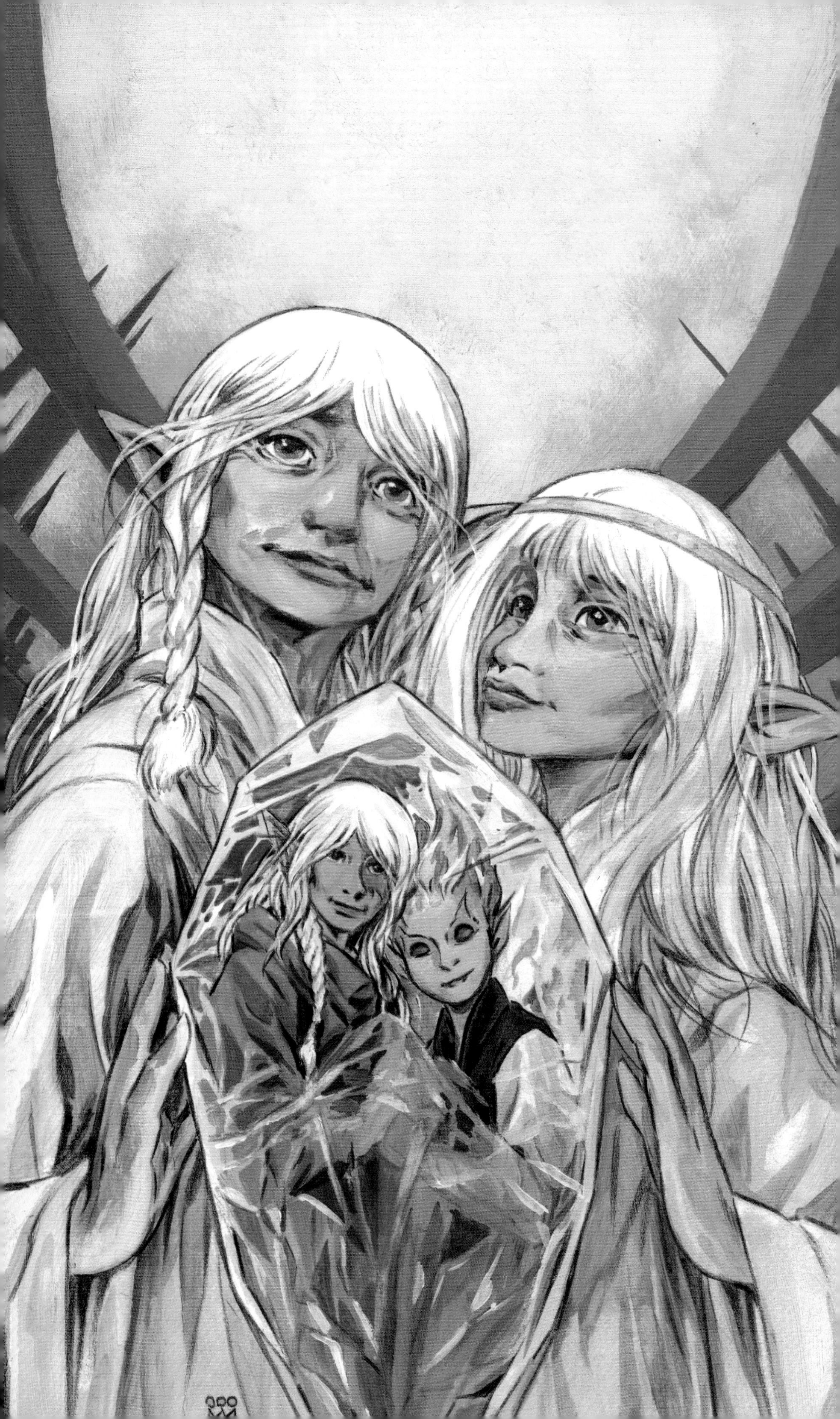

THE DARK CRYSTAL SKETCHBOOK

Under the guidance of The Jim Henson Company, Kelly and Nichole Matthews designed Thurma and the Firelings based on original concept art by Brian Froud. The following pages offer a behind-the-scenes look at the process.

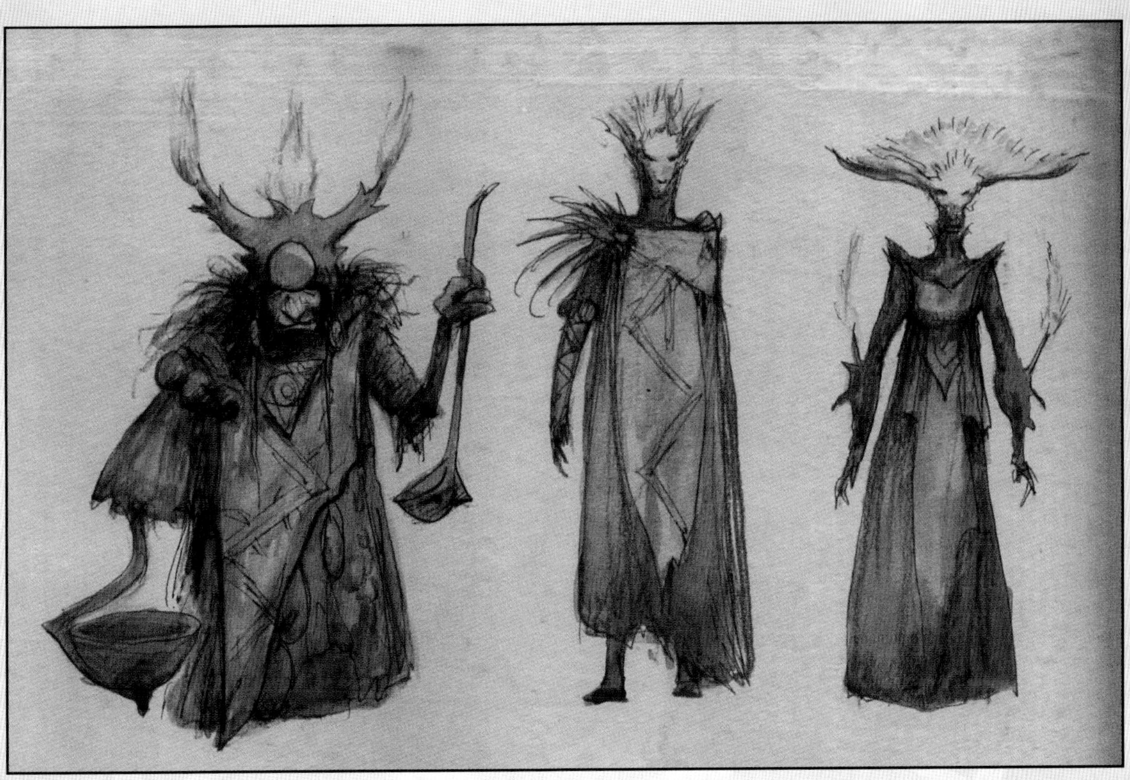

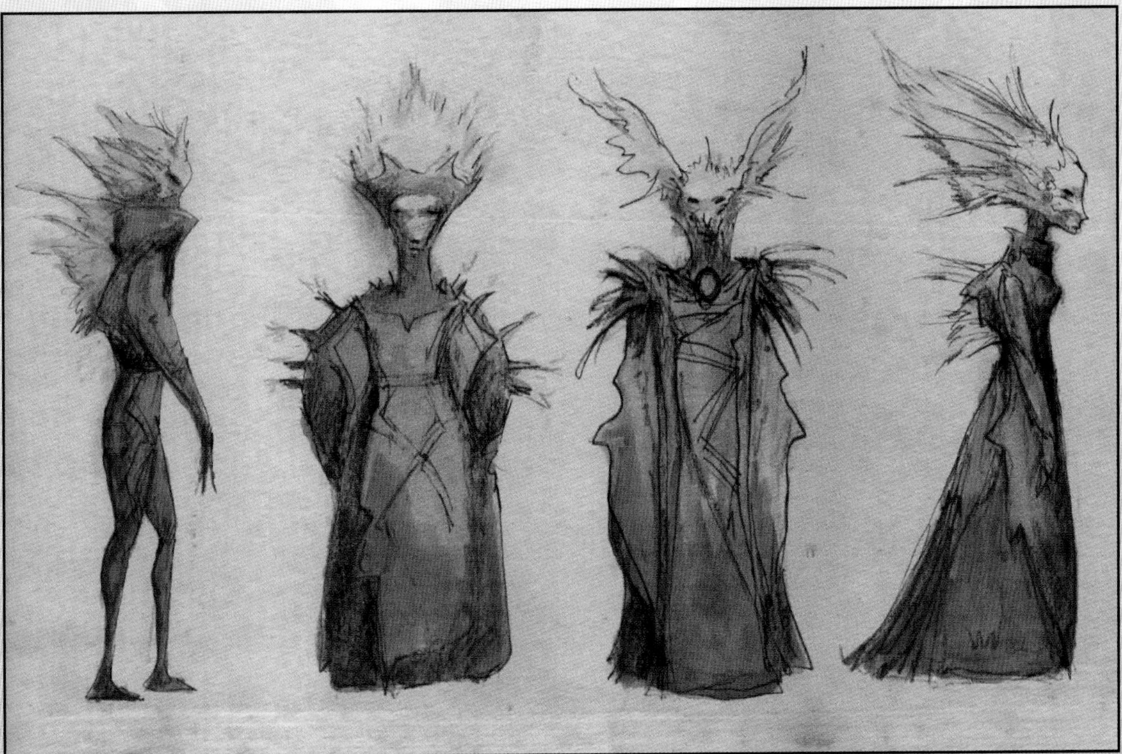

Original Fireling concept art by Brian Froud.

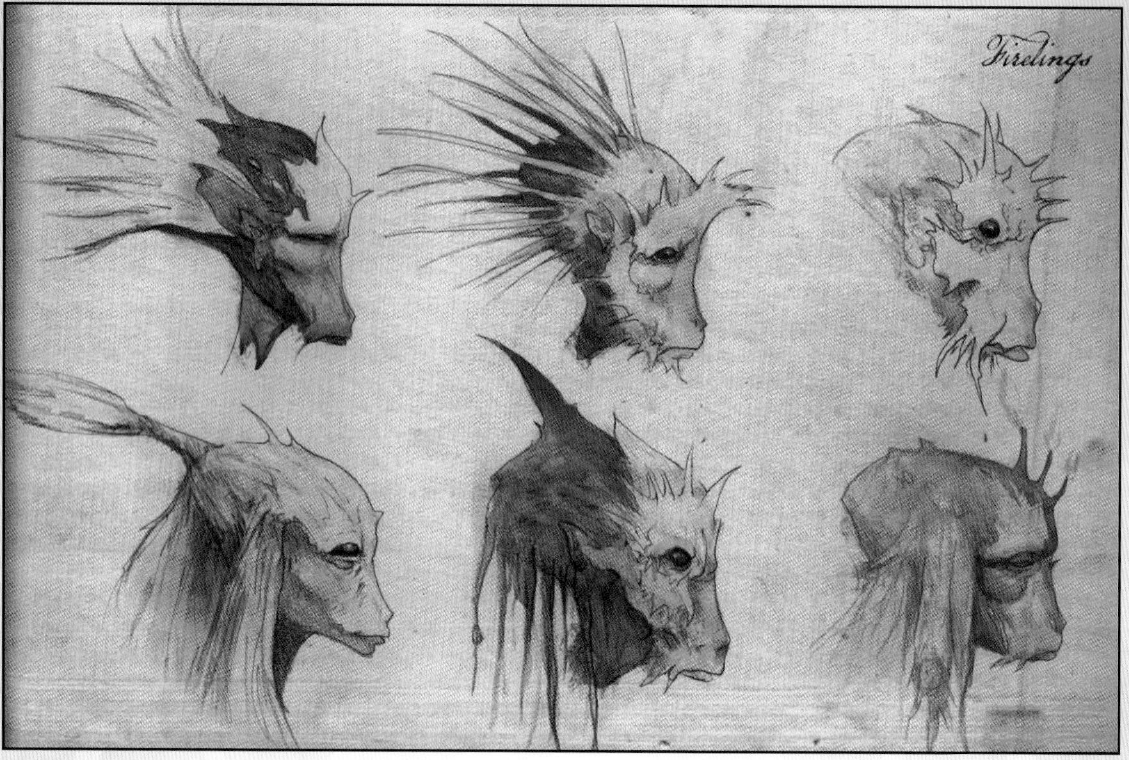
Firelings

Original Fireling headshot concept art by Brian Froud.

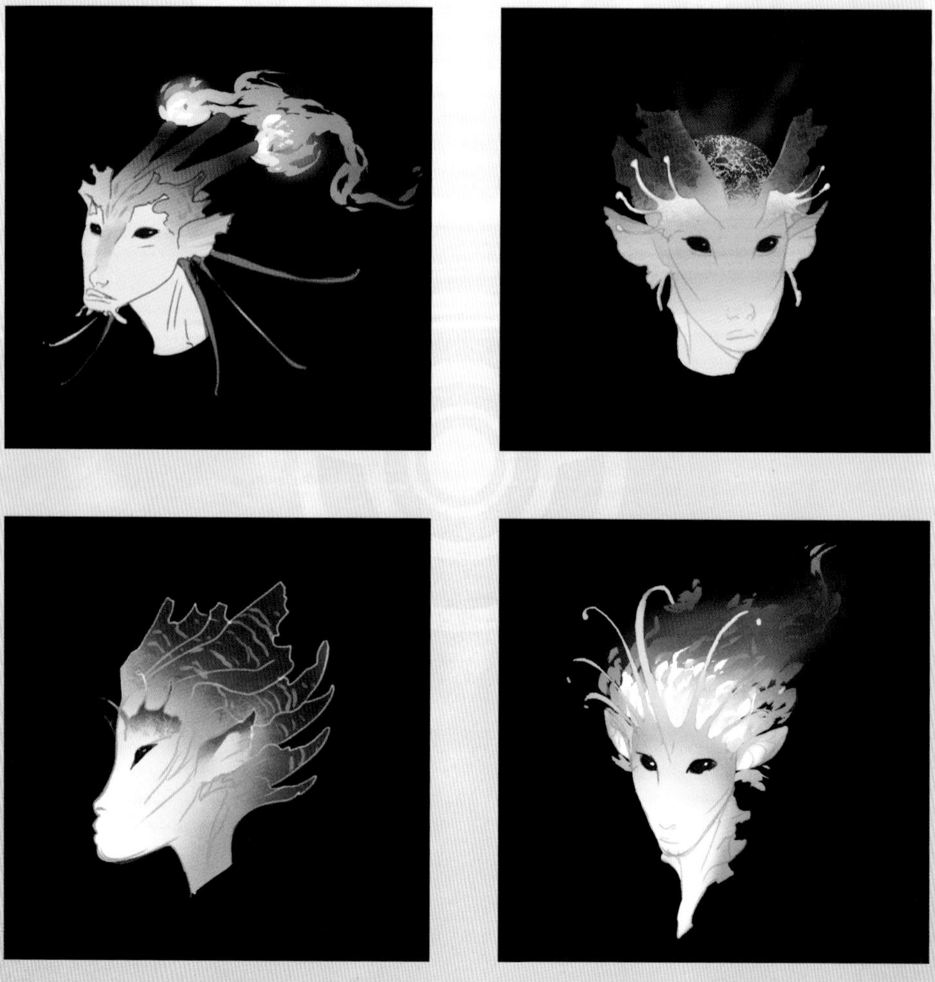

Fireling design process by Kelly and Nichole Matthews, based on Brian Froud's concept art.

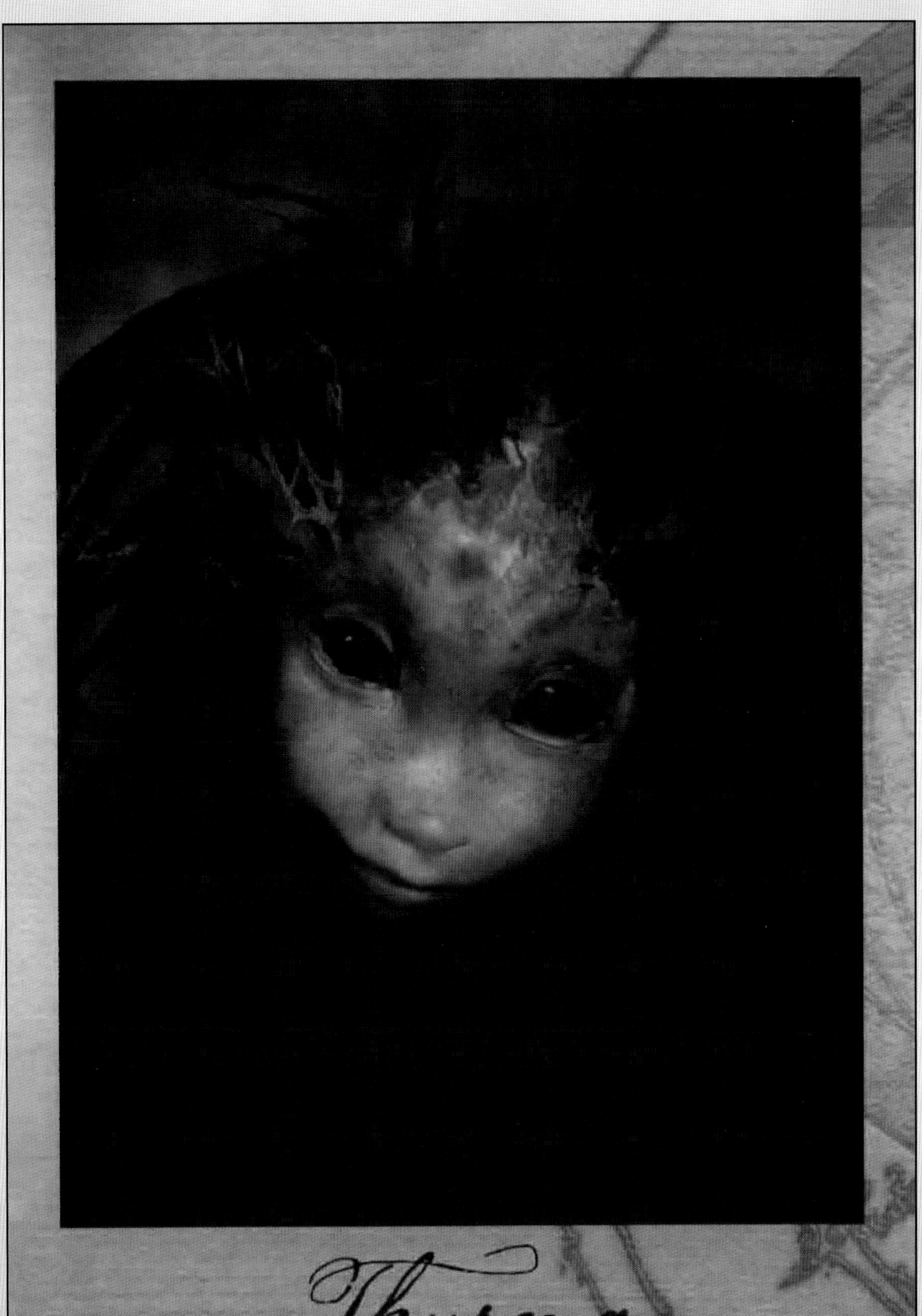
Thurma

Original Thurma concept art by Brian Froud and Wendy Froud.

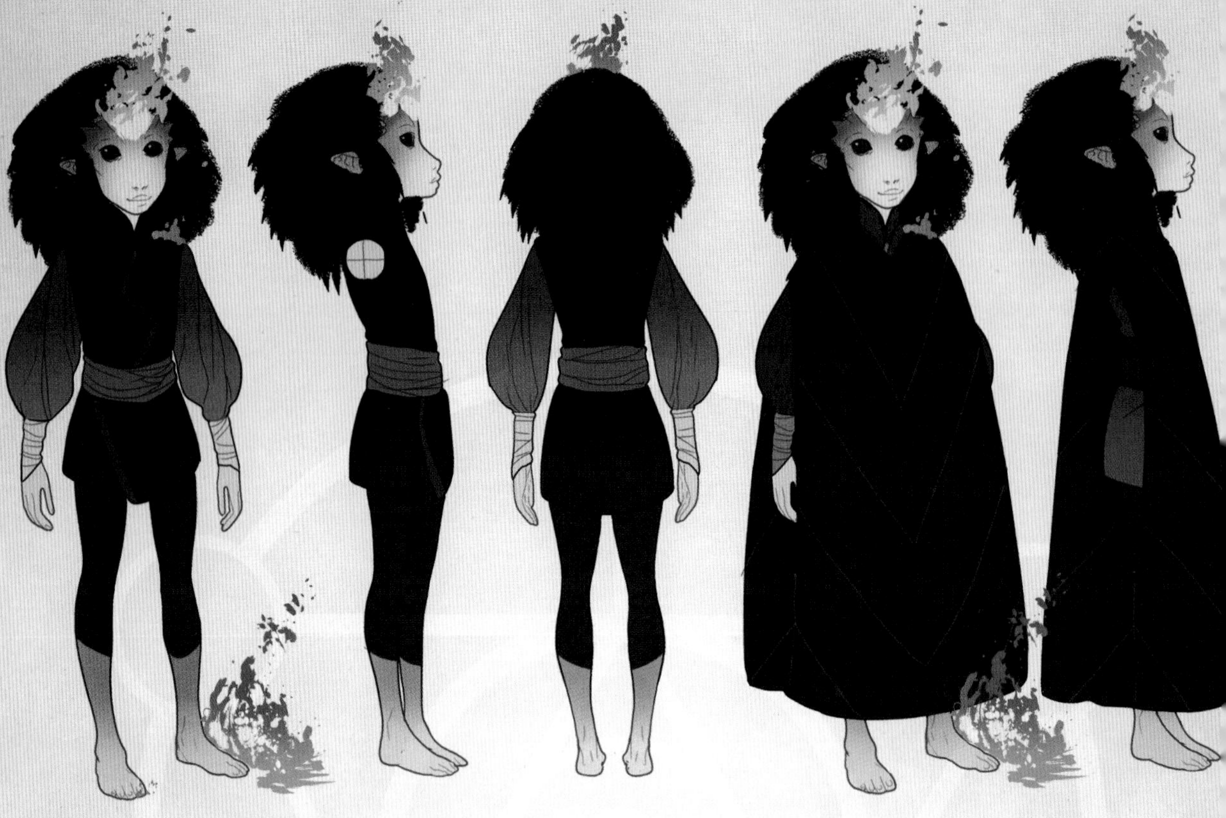

First pass on the Thurma character design by Kelly and Nichole Matthews.

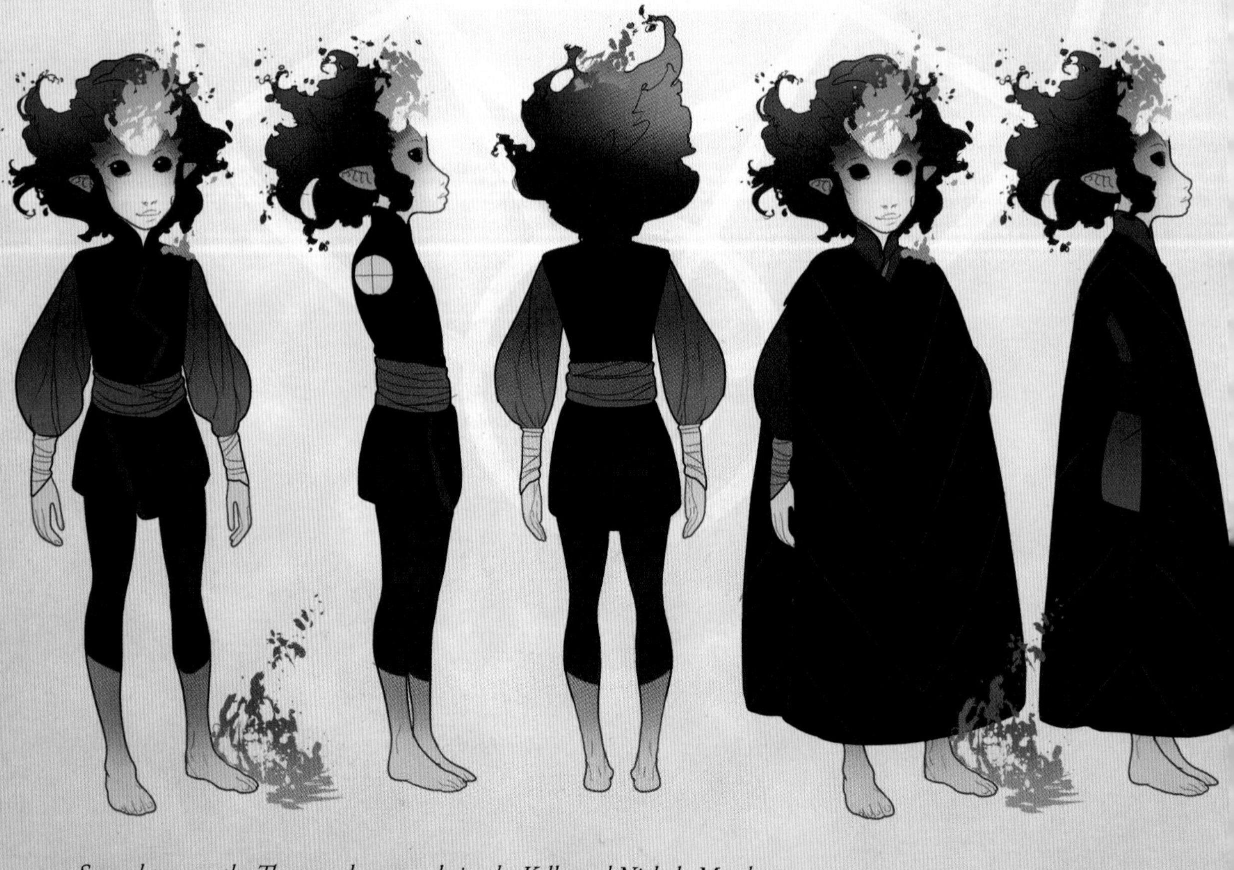

Second pass on the Thurma character design by Kelly and Nichole Matthews.

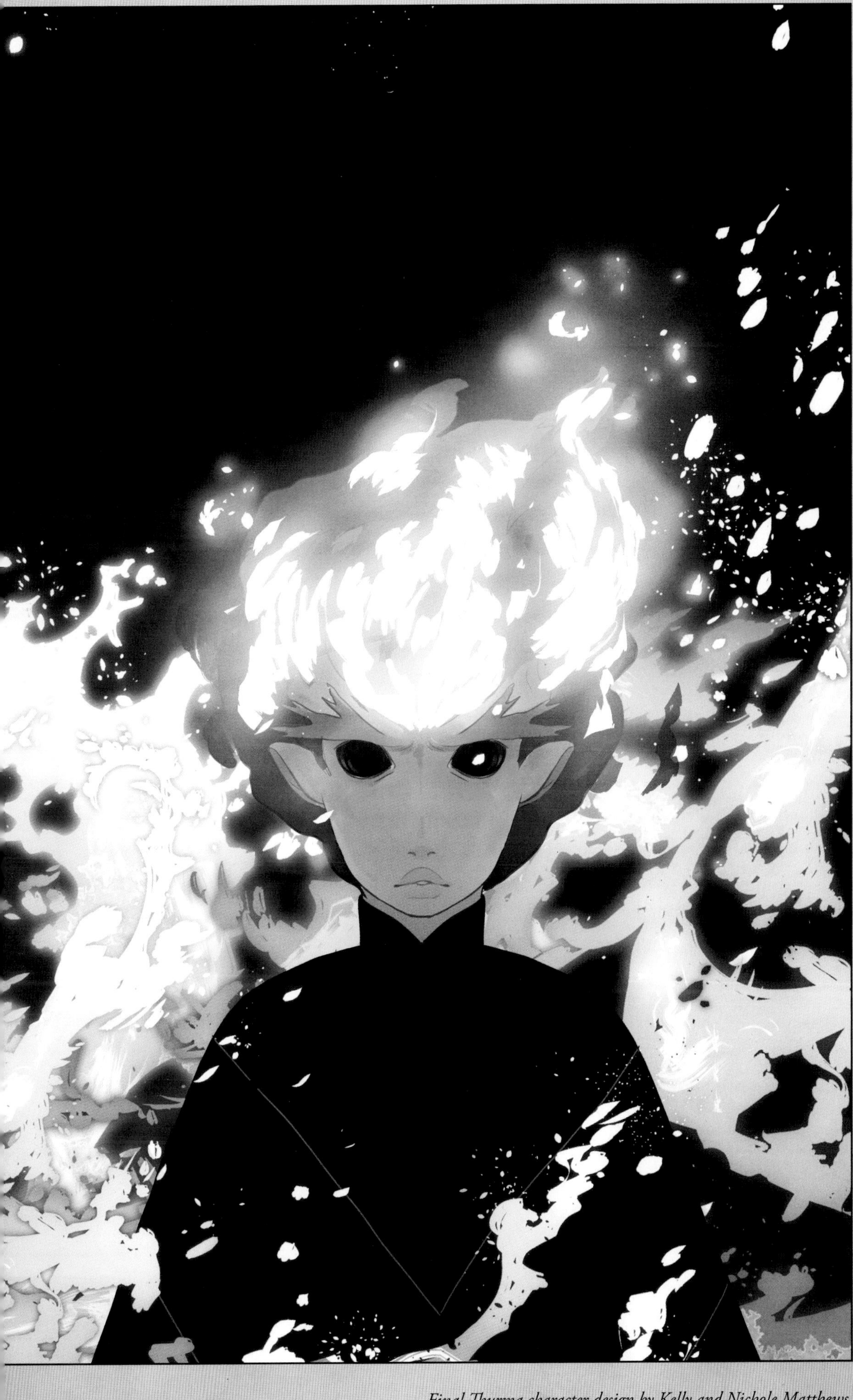

Final Thurma character design by Kelly and Nichole Matthews.

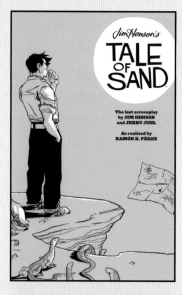